# MALE
# ARMOR

Cultural Frames, Framing Culture

*Robert Newman, Editor*

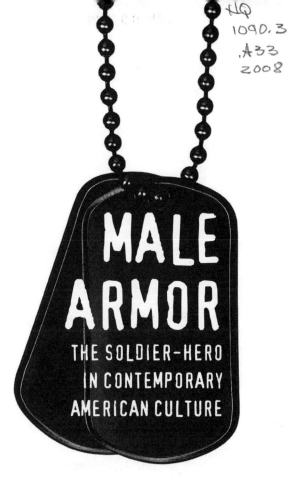

# MALE ARMOR

## THE SOLDIER-HERO IN CONTEMPORARY AMERICAN CULTURE

## JON ROBERT ADAMS

University of Virginia Press

*Charlottesville and London*

University of Virginia Press
© 2008 by the Rector and Visitors of the University of Virginia
Printed in the United States of America on acid-free paper

*First published 2008*

9 8 7 6 5 4 3 2 1

Library of Congress Cataloging-in-Publication Data
Adams, Jon Robert, 1968–
   Male armor : the soldier-hero in contemporary American culture / Jon Robert
   Adams.
       p.     cm. — (Cultural frames, framing culture)
   Includes bibliographical references and index.
   ISBN 978-0-8139-2752-7 (cloth : alk. paper) — ISBN 978-0-8139-2753-4 (pbk. :
alk. paper)
   1. Men—United States. 2. Masculinity—United States. 3. War in literature.
4. Masculinity in literature. I. Title.
   HQ1090.3.A33 2008
   305.310973—dc22
                                      2008003090

*to Mom and Dad*
*for all the right beginnings*

*and to Dave*
*for everything*
*every day*

# CONTENTS

# ACKNOWLEDGMENTS

Over the dozen or so years of my work on this project, I have benefited immensely from the counsel, editing, proofreading, and sage advice of so many friends and colleagues that either recollecting or recompensing them fully seems nearly impossible. My desire to offer some semblance of thanks, however, prompts me to at least try here. I beg forgiveness of anyone I have inadvertently forgotten.

My thoughts about these subjects began during my baccalaureate career and crystallized as I obtained my master's degree, so I begin by thanking early personal and professional mentors Alanna Kathleen Brown, professor emerita of Montana State University, and Veronica Stewart, professor emerita of the University of Montana. My writing on issues of gender began during my doctoral studies at the University of California, Riverside (UCR), and culminated in my qualifying examinations and dissertation, directed by Katherine Kinney and advised by Steven Axelrod, the late Phillip Brett, Emory Elliott, and George Haggerty. UCR also offered me a generous dissertation fellowship that allowed me to complete some of the work that would become this book.

During a postdoctoral fellowship at the University of California, Davis, as I began to consider a book-length project, I learned a great deal from the editorial and organizational advice of my faculty mentor, Elizabeth Freeman. I garnered other intellectual wealth from Gerry Brenner, professor emeritus of the University of Montana, and the late Gregory Bredbeck of the University of California, Riverside.

My colleagues at Western Michigan University (WMU) have been nothing less than instrumental in seeing this book to fruition, so I'd like to thank first my faculty reading group, which discussed an early proposal for the project for an entire evening: Beth Bradburn, Meg Dupuis, Steve Feffer, Lisa Minnick, and Chris Nagle. Nic Witschi encouraged me not only to consider a book project but also to pitch it to acquisitions editors at the Modern Language Association conference. Acting above and beyond the call of duty, he then proofread and responded to my initial book proposal. Todd Kuchta helped me shape a more cohesive and intelligible introduction. Along the way Patti Bills, Tony Ellis, Arnie Johnston, Katherine Joslin, Cynthia Klekar, Jil Larson, Casey McKittrick, John Saillant, Eve Salisbury, Jana Schulman, Scott Slawinski, Gwen Tarbox, Charie Thralls, Grace Tiffany, Karen Vocke, Joyce Walker, Allen Webb, and Lance Weldy variously offered support, compliments, encouragement, indispensable reading, and professional advice. The English Department office administrative staff, Becky Beech, Michelle Hruska, and Bethlynn Sanders, mitigated the traumas of everyday working life.

Additionally, I would like to thank Zaydun Al-Shara and Noah Hilgert for research assistance when I did not have the time for it. And I owe an enormous debt of gratitude to Erin Kenzie for listening, researching, arguing, and editing, and for the best formatting skills a Luddite could desire.

Cathie Brettschneider, humanities acquisitions editor at the University of Virginia Press, expressed an early interest in this project and facilitated its many steps to publication. Ellen Satrom, managing editor, helped me sort out acknowledgments, permissions, and formatting details. I received absolutely invaluable advice from the two anonymous reviewers of the manuscript, and with her copy-editing expertise, Carol Sickman-Garner made me a better writer. Sally Hawthorne assiduously prepared the index, and the generous support of Western Michigan University's PPP&E fund helped me finalize the manuscript. I only hope that this published product warrants the time and attention they paid to it. Its shortcomings, however, are entirely my own.

I would never have come to the readings of the texts compiled here without the experience of having taught them to a number of different classes. So heartfelt thanks to the students of ENGL 146 at the University of California, Davis, fall 2002 (and to Catherine Fung, my teaching assistant); ENGL 522 at Western Michigan University, fall 2003; and ENGL 555 at Western Michigan University, spring 2004. I'd like to acknowledge in particular spring 2007's WMU students of ENGL 5400, who read many of the books featured in this project as I revised it and who confirmed my thoughts and, innocently unaware of their stunning brilliance, completely obliterated them at the same time. If they are the future of scholarship on gender, war, and American national identity, perhaps we can avoid some of the pitfalls described herein.

Portions of this book have been printed elsewhere in modified form. I would like to credit, with many thanks, *Harrington's Gay Male Fiction Quarterly*, in which parts of chapter 1 were published as "'The Great General Was a Has-Been': Homoerotic Re-definitions of Masculinity in 1950's Conformist Culture" (vol. 6, no. 3, 2004). *Studies in American Culture* published a shorter version of chapter 3 as "Upholding Masculinity in Michael Herr's *Dispatches* and David Rabe's *Streamers*" (vol. 28, no. 2, 2005). The editors of these journals, Thomas L. Long and Robert L. McDonald, respectively, were of pivotal importance in guiding the articles to publication and were gracious to allow their reprinting here.

Finally, I'd like to acknowledge the personal and emotional support of many friends and family, without whom I wouldn't be the scholar or the person that I am. So for all your encouragement, love, and unflagging support, thanks to Steve and Marnie Adams (and Anthony, Allison, and Alexandra), the extended Adams family, the extended Alig family, Richard Anderson, Corinne Archibald, Dick Geist, the extended Heck family, Marcy Newman, and Bill and Lisa Wheeler (and Abigail and Jacob).

# MALE
# ARMOR

# SOLDIER'S
# HEART

**American war literature has, at its best, depicted the violence of war to challenge popular assumptions.**
—Marilyn Wesley, *Violent Adventure: Contemporary Fiction by American Men*

Marilyn Wesley suggests that the best American war literature serves as an intermediary between the event that inspires the violent depictions and cultural assumptions about that event. *Male Armor* intends to show another way that representations of American wars function as an intermediary, in this case between the male soldier's experience of war and civilian beliefs about his masculinity. This book investigates the bifurcation and persistent tension between American conceptions of masculinity and the soldierly experience of war as evident in literary, dramatic, filmic, and nonfiction portrayals of the United States' late twentieth-century conflicts. The project focuses specifically on war representations because of war's contradictory function in the American imaginary as both guarantor of and threat to manhood. After a century that charted a general loosening of the strictures on manhood, war continues to represent, in the civilian mindset that some soldiers bring to their service, an antidote to the effeminization of American men, at most, and a means to achieve manhood, at least. This book demonstrates that though the specific war texts *Male Armor* studies mark altering perceptions of masculinity in the culture at large, they also continuously resist the popular American compunction to equate manhood with soldierly function. By suggesting that many other representations of war may function as the texts studied here do, *Male Armor* hopes to offer a long-overdue corrective to the idea that war makes men and to interrogate the United States' time-honored link between its sense of national self and the performance of American men at war. As the texts studied here demonstrate, war provides society with definitions of manhood, while, simultaneously, men experience war as the antithesis of society's definition. Something has to break somewhere, and it's usually the men.

A 1 March 2005 PBS *Frontline* documentary entitled "The Soldier's Heart" portrays the effects of Operation Iraqi Freedom on veterans and consequently reveals the bifurcation at the center of *Male Armor:* the disparity between soldiers' experiences and civilian American conceptions of soldierly masculinity. The documentary recounts the mental and emotional repercussions of Operation Iraqi Freedom on several U.S. military servicemen and investigates the attempts of various branches of the military to handle these repercussions. During and after their service all of the soldiers featured in the documentary exhibited medical, psychological, and/or behavioral responses regularly associated with symptoms of post-traumatic stress disorder (PTSD), ranging from suicidal or murderous thoughts and actions, to depression and anxiety, to alcohol addictions and hallucinations.[1] One soldier, Jeff Lucey, of the Marine Reserves of the Sixth Motor Transport Battalion, committed suicide by hanging himself with a garden hose ten months after his return from a tour of duty in Iraq. Another, twenty-two-year-old Jacob Martin, a machine gunner with the First Marine Division, describes the day when his "brain snapped" and he woke up with "everything different." He began to spend long periods of time staring at walls and contemplating various ways to harm both himself and others with his marine-issue weapons. Army Special Forces interrogator Staff Sergeant Andrew Pogany became immobilized after seeing the burned-out, mutilated body of an Iraqi on only his second day in country.

While the responses of these soldiers may not initially surprise, perhaps because deleterious psychological responses to trauma seem expected, even commonplace to the public at large, the accounts of their misgivings about seeking help most certainly do. Despite their differences in age, military branch, service history, and rank, none of the soldiers found asking for help uncomplicated. Andrew Pomerantz, M.D., chief of mental health services for the Veterans Administration (VA) in Vermont, says that "the stigma to receiving mental health services inside the military is huge," and he claims that "the biggest barrier . . . is being thought of as a wimp." Moreover, Pomerantz continues, those who consider seeking treatment "actually fear retribution and punishment if they express psychological distress" ("Soldier's Heart").

For example, Jeff Lucey, fearing that his unit's discovery of his request would entail their loss of faith in him or worse, refused Veterans Administration assistance for months, even once he learned that the VA was not a part of the military and would not share his records with the Marine Reserves. Under imminent danger of harming himself, Lucey eventually entered treatment at a VA hospital, but his release forms, filled out just three days later, indicate that the threat he presented to himself had abated. Telling his girlfriend that he wanted to "come home and drink," Lucey left the VA's care and subsequently killed himself. In between deployments Martin likewise acknowledged his need for professional assistance in coping with violent fantasies. Subsequently, he sought mental health help from the marines at Camp Pendleton, to which he had returned for training prior to a scheduled redeployment to Iraq. Martin was ridiculed by his fellow soldiers and discouraged from joining a newly formed support group for postcombat trauma sufferers, part of what the marines call "resiliency training" ("Soldier's Heart"). Concerned about his ability to function upon his return to Iraq and determined to rid himself of psychological afflictions, Martin joined the group nonetheless, only to have the self-same hecklers later inquire whether or not the therapy had seemed to help. In perhaps the most egregious case the documentary recounts, Pogany was harassed by his superiors and fellow soldiers, removed from his combat post, and eventually indicted by the army for cowardly conduct.

All the *Frontline* documentary cases demonstrate the military's accession to the need for mental health assistance for combat veterans. As Lieutenant Colonel Dave Grossman of the U.S. Army, now retired, indicates, the military has long known of the deleterious mental health effects of combat. In an invited lecture at Camp Pendleton, Grossman told soldiers that "on any given day" in the United States' three major twentieth-century wars—

World Wars I and II and Korea—the military "had more psychiatric casualties than all the ones killed by the enemy" ("Soldier's Heart").

But events like Grossman's lecture are not part of the marines' regular training, and Pogany's case in particular manifests the military's painfully slow progress in not only implementing avenues for help but also changing individual and organizational attitudes toward soldiers' attempts to secure such help. Pogany initially reported his anxiety to his unit commander, saying that he couldn't "turn off" his reluctance sufficiently to commence his duties. He sought the assistance of one of the "Combat Stress Control Teams" in Iraq, employed during Operation Iraqi Freedom for the first time in U.S. military history. After a brief interview the Control Team recommended the standard three-day reprieve from combat for Pogany so that he could relax at the rear of operations, get more counseling, and return to active status mentally prepared. Pogany's immediate supervisor, a sergeant major, refused the recommendation and used various epithets for Pogany, from "failure" to "coward." Pogany was ordered to stay away from his fellow soldiers so as not to infect them with his cowardice and, in front of a Control Team psychologist, was told that fifty years ago the U.S. Army Special Reserves would have taken wimps like him out and shot them. The threat resembles the darkly comic terror Joseph Heller evokes in *Catch-22* when Colonel Cathcart orders Major Danby to be taken out and shot for moaning during a briefing. Even "the two young lieutenants" ordered to carry out the shooting "nodded lumpishly and gaped at each other in stunned and flaccid reluctance" (Heller 232). Heller defuses the tension and prevents the shooting via a characteristic blip that alters the course of events, but his need to do so comically only renders the tragedy of Pogany's experience that much more egregious. After repeated and escalating harassment Pogany was returned to his deployment base, from which the army initiated cowardly conduct investigative proceedings, eventually charging Pogany with violating Article 99 of the Uniform Code of Military Justice—cowardly conduct as a result of fear—a violation punishable by death.[2]

The introduction of support groups at Camp Pendleton and Combat Stress Control Teams in Operation Iraqi Freedom indicates the military's clear progress in attempting to care for soldiers exhibiting mental and emotional trauma, though such changes proceed glacially, and institutional and attitudinal resistance remains. According to Jonathan Shay, a psychiatrist and the author of *Odysseus in America*, a study of combat veterans returning to civilian life, "There are plenty of things that happen right inside the Pentagon that never get out to the file in terms of actually influencing people's beliefs and behavior" ("Soldier's Heart"). Additionally, many soldiers continue to fear retribution for any attempt to secure mental health assistance. The *Frontline* documentary claims that "when the Army did their own survey of troops serving in Iraq, nearly half of those most in need of psychological help reported that they felt if they asked for such help, their leaders would blame them for the problem, that they would be seen as weak and that their unit would have less confidence in them."

Of all the "Soldier's Heart" examples, Jacob Martin was the most persistent in getting help. That he was also the youngest soldier in the program's survey perhaps signals a more progressive societal acceptance of the effects of psychological trauma and a stronger reluctance to stigmatize those who seek care among younger generations. Perhaps the days of shooting "wimps" and sentencing cowards to death are indeed over. Nevertheless, with over one million soldiers serving or having served in present-day conflicts in Iraq and Afghanistan, estimates that as many as one in six will suffer PTSD certainly underscore that the military's successful inculcation of new practices for and changed attitudes about mental health likely cannot come quickly enough.

Unfortunately, careful scrutiny of the largely positive shifts in approaches to treating psychologically damaged soldiers reveals persistent, onerous connections between a soldier's ability to function and his perceived manhood. The *Frontline* stories catalog how individual servicemembers react vehemently to their affected subordinates or peers and use well-established gendered and/or sexual epithets to denigrate them—pansy, sissy, pussy, faggot. These responses suggest that American cultural expectations about gender continue to inform demands for mental stability. Such reactions reiterate the time-honored connection between men and rationality that seems anachronistic in contemporary society and dangerous in branches of the military integrated by gender. With increasingly visible places and roles for women, the U.S. military seems poised, at the opening of the twenty-first century, to account for changes in cultural conceptions of gender and gender function.[3] Yet on an individual attitudinal level that permeates the entire institution sufficiently enough to discourage psychologically damaged soldiers from identifying themselves, some soldiers, including commanding officers in the *Frontline* example, often revert to outmoded, either/or binary constructions of manhood that dictate what men are and how they behave. When seen through the lens of mental health, military policy changes indicated by the *Frontline* documentary reflect an attempt to account for increasingly complex understandings of gender. But the attitudes of individual soldiers are often slow to accommodate the alternative viewpoints that subtend changes in policy, and these attitudes are entrenched in and supported by the civilian public at large. On some fronts we appear to have progressed; on others we have significant work ahead in unifying attitudes, policy, and practice.

I introduce the "Soldier's Heart" example not to fault the U.S. military for its sluggish progress in accommodating mental health concerns or for its incomplete integration of women into service, but to depict in microcosm a present-day example of the tension between the male experience of war and societal conceptions of masculinity. Other such microcosmic depictions of this tension emerge throughout *Male Armor*—in the introductions to analyses in the chapters and in the epigraphs preceding them. This tension, though slightly altered in detail and progressively changing over the last fifty years (what I call "contemporary America" in this study), permeates representations of war since World War II to the extent that it has become an almost necessary attribute for representing war. In my readings select texts such as the World War II novels of Norman Mailer, James Jones, and Joseph Heller, and plays, films, and memoirs about Vietnam, Desert Storm, and present-day Iraq and Afghanistan, stand as attempts to rectify gaps in understanding among American culture's beliefs about war and men, military expectations of the soldier, and the soldier's experience of combat. These gaps appear largely responsible not only for soldiers' treacherous reintegration into civilian society, which the *Frontline* documentary highlights, but also, as I will argue, for continuing support of the war enterprise. The texts *Male Armor* studies (and potentially many others) continually demonstrate both soldiers' disillusionment with manhood as the promise of war and their difficulty articulating how they have been unmade by war to a culture still enthralled by its perceived promise. By locating both historically and culturally the discursive tensions that have given rise to and exploited gaps between civilians and soldiers, *Male Armor* hopes to offer a way to interpret and understand textual representations of war and to intervene in the American public's continued investment in the war enterprise as a guarantor of masculinity and, by extension, of the nation.

In titling this introduction, I have intentionally reverted to Civil War tax-onomy for the afflictions soldiers experience postwar: "soldier's heart." The biological and psychological maladies currently (and likely temporarily) grouped under the general heading "post-traumatic stress disorder" have, in each twentieth-century war era, obtained new nomenclature. In World War I soldiers suffered "shell-shock." Remaining deployed "for the duration" of World War II brought on the ailments then called "battle fatigue." And only significantly after the 1975 fall of Saigon did the Veterans Administra-tion add PTSD to the list of post-Vietnam combat-related diseases. Unlike the Civil War label, however, each of the twentieth-century names identi-fies a cause *external* to the body as responsible for the soldiers' reactions, and these attributions certainly signal something about our expectations for the resiliency of men.[4] Like the *Frontline* documentary, then, *Male Armor* asks: what changes might materialize were we to always favor internal ef-fects over external influences when we conceptualize masculinity or when we justify war?

### The Persistent Gap

**They're so good at making soldiers, but they're not as good at making men.**
—10,000 Maniacs, "Gun Shy"

Natalie Merchant's lyrics to "Gun Shy," a song ostensibly about the return of her "baby brother Jude" from boot camp, present a civilian understanding of the relationship between war and masculinity that *Male Armor* hopes to encourage, an understanding that unlinks soldiering from definitions of manhood. Whereas Merchant derisively faults the military "they," this book hopes to intervene between civilians and their ideas about war by examining how contemporary representations of war in American culture persistently foreground disjunctions between soldierly experience of war and civilian attitudes toward it. Among these attitudes is the time-honored notion that war makes men. If, as Joshua Goldstein contends, "cultures use gender in constructing social roles that enable war" (251), then *Male Armor* hopes to use representations of war to show how gender fails to function in accord with expectations of it. The study suggests that only by revealing fictions in social constructions of gender can we hope to disable war. Three elements thus emerge as important to establish how this book's analysis will unfold: (1) traditional definitions of masculinity as the culture invests in them; (2) connections between those definitions and ideas about war; and (3) the myriad ways that soldierly experience of war, as portrayed in selected late twentieth-century representations of it, consistently resists or negates the definitions of manhood that civilian culture attaches to war.

The first of these elements, traditionally defined masculinity, is perhaps the easiest to comprehend—everyone knows what a man is—yet also the most difficult to pin down or exemplify. In pondering masculinity's paradoxical status as both omnipresent and nebulous, John MacInness asks, "Why is it that masculinity is an obvious concept which must therefore have a real social existence (so that people can readily produce lists of what it comprises and these lists are remarkably consistent), yet is incapable of any precise empirical definition, such that people will reject these same lists as useful or accurate descriptions of empirically existing men?" (15).

Lists such as those MacInness describes often feature both attributes and actions. For example, Michael Schwalbe says that "a man must show that he is rational, tough, indomitable, ambitious, competitive, in control, able to get a job done and ardently heterosexual" (18). And David Buchbinder claims that "men are generally shown to be stoic, bearing their agony discreetly, dismissing mortal wounds as mere scratches, and thinking of others—family, girlfriend, home, another soldier—rather than themselves" (75). Upon close examination, however, the lists betray the fact that attributes consistent with traditional masculinity can only be *revealed* via men's actions, which prompts Buchbinder to conclude, summarily, that "masculine is what men in their immense variety *do*" (2, emphasis in original), not necessarily or entirely who they *are*.

But masculinity has also long been defined by what it is *not*, in other words, through a system of binary oppositions, including man/woman, male/female, and masculine/feminine. Roger Horrocks calls the cultural meaning derived from these binaries masculinity's "unitary function" and insists that "all shades of masculine identity, ranging from macho to the effeminate, have this in common: they convey the message: 'I am not a woman'" (*Masculinity* 33). Buchbinder extends the binary divisions in the categories of sex and gender to include sexuality: "the category of the masculine is . . . produced discursively by a double movement, which defines the masculine first in terms of sex—male, as against female—and then in terms of sexuality—heterosexual, as against homosexual" (64). Hence arises the insistence on "ardently heterosexual" actions in Schwalbe's classifying system quoted above.

According to Judith Butler, the signifying systems of gender maintain their power via a process that roughly follows the trajectory of inclusion—oppression—exclusion. Butler writes that "the economy that claims to include the feminine as the subordinate term in a binary opposition of masculine/feminine excludes the feminine, produces the feminine as that which must be excluded for that economy to operate" (*Bodies* 36). Since masculine cannot exist without its opposite, against which it is defined, the feminine is included, Butler argues, only to be excluded in service of masculinity's maintenance of power. And Susan Jeffords notes that though "the composition of the masculine can vary from time to time, it remains consistently opposed to the 'feminine,' those characteristics that must be discarded in order to actualize masculinity" (*Remasculinization* xiii).

Certainly, as much of human history attests, war provides a pivotal arena for actualizing masculinity, perhaps precisely because it historically excludes women and with them ostensibly anything feminine. Joshua Goldstein points out that "a uniform pattern . . . links men with war-fighting in every society that fights wars" (10). The pattern is so pervasive that it prompts Sam Keen to write that "the male psyche is, first and foremost, the warrior psyche" (37). And Jeffords continues that "the crystallized formations of masculinity in warfare . . . enable gender relations in society to survive" (*Remasculinization* xiv).

*Male Armor* labels as "soldierly masculinity" the particular brand of traditional male function associated with heroism—courage, suppressed emotion, strength, and clearheaded decisiveness, attributes that, Joshua Goldstein concludes, "cultures develop [to] equate manhood with toughness under fire" and to "help overcome soldiers' reluctance to fight" (9). Men who exhibit these behaviors are soldier-heroes. Men who do not are not seen as men. As the *Frontline* examples show, these cultural expectations of soldierly masculinity persist as the most reified, most pernicious, and least challenged of any of the functions of gender. Yet even cursory examination of cultural productions that feature war as a subject elicits myriad examples of men who do not experience war or soldiering as beneficial to their sense of manliness and who are or become, in the traditional sense, failed men. Such texts, among which *Male Armor* analyzes a select few, become fertile ground for considering whether a disruption in cultural understandings about gender could initiate changes in civilian attitudes about war.

But the tradition of linking manhood to war—of in fact making the former dependent upon the latter—enjoys time-honored status in cultures all over of the world. Given the numerous exceptions to soldierly masculinity featured in representations of war, the tenacity of civilian definitions of heroic masculinity becomes glaring, surprising, and unfortunate. One auspicious example that sets the stage for *Male Armor*'s contemporary view emerges in late nineteenth-century American culture, which witnessed a dramatic upheaval in social and domestic power relations. Barely recovered from the economically damaging Civil War, the United States entered a period of unprecedented growth and modernization precipitated by two divergent yet related forces: the closing of the American frontier and industrialization. The former relegated the notion of perpetual westward expansion to the American imagination and created nostalgic images of a way of life and modes of interaction that still, a century later, haunt cultural consciousness and exact a toll on American systems of belief. Concomitantly, industrialization ushered in hitherto unimaginable alterations in American culture by granting Americans a newfound mobility and ease of labor and by fueling a mass exodus from the rural, agrarian lifestyle. These forces in turn created modern urbanization and, eventually, the American middle class. Michael Messner calls these changes "modernization" collectively, which, he says, "was characterized by the closing of the frontier, industrialization, urbanization, [and] the rise of modern bureaucracies" (9). Sons left their fathers' farms and relocated to cities in order to secure positions in the businesses and factories forged by industrialization. Scott Derrick observes that "the ongoing transformation of the nineteenth-century economy, fueled by forces such as geographical mobility, urbanization, and explosive population growth, meant that sons would often find work in positions that barely existed as possibilities for older generations" (8).

The urbanization of agrarian America that Derrick and others describe, however, was not without its consequences, particularly for the psyches of America's sons, who had replaced the quest for a new life on the frontier with moves to the city. Many rural Americans still clung to Victorian prudishness and believed that cities housed moral and sexual temptations to which young men would fall prey. Considering professional work inactive and therefore harmful to young men's manhood, many also decried the new employment young men sought in business and factories. Agriculture constituted the American economy up to the Industrial Revolution, and the yeoman farmer who earned a living through hard labor on the land was the ideal American. Some observers of American culture began to fear that young men were becoming overcivilized by life in the cities, and they associated overcivilization with emasculation (Seltzer 153; Rotundo 251).

Coupled with the tendency to view nascent urban occupations as inferior to vigorous subsistence work was the overarching concern that American boys had already been feminized by Victorian culture's separation of the social and domestic spheres, which dictated that much of a young boy's life was spent almost entirely in the company of women. George Chauncey asserts that "politicians, businessmen, educators, and sportsmen alike protested the dangers of 'overcivilization' to American manhood and thus to American culture, in a not very oblique reference to the dangers of women's civilizing influence and the effeminization of men" (113).

So fearful of the feminizing influences of women or of civilization were many male leaders that they founded a spate of sports, clubs, and outdoor organizations meant to "free young males from women, especially mothers" (Dubbert 152). The role of such groups, according to Chauncey, was to "restore the role of men in the socialization of youth" (113). Among the organizations spawned were the Knights of King Arthur, the Sons of Daniel Boone, and in 1912 the Boy Scouts of America (Chauncey 113).

Amid the well-intentioned efforts to socialize America's boys, American men, influenced by sweeping economic and social change, also faced uncertainty when defining the new century's masculinity and the codes pertaining thereto. By 1900, Joe Dubbert argues, masculine identity was becoming "more and more confusing," and anxiety over American masculinity culminated in misgivings about the nation's defense. Efforts to quell apprehensions over the demise of manhood imbued dialogues concerning the health of the nation. Preeminent among politicians concerned with the state of American masculinity was Theodore Roosevelt. Fresh from his experience as a Rough Rider in the Spanish-American War, Roosevelt believed in the interdependent health of men and the nation; an effeminized, weakened male populace could not, he felt, defend the nation. George Chauncey claims that "the quest for manhood became the central metaphorical image in [Roosevelt's] speeches, which cast the struggle of national revitalization and international supremacy as a struggle for manhood itself" (113). To this end Roosevelt advocated manly practices by placing himself at the center of what came to be called a "cult of muscularity" (Chauncey 116) and encouraged outdoor activity by founding the U.S. Forest Service. Joe Dubbert concludes that "the point stuck in the minds of nineteenth-century men that a physical life in the open air was far more enhancing to masculinity than a constricted life and a vocation in a city" (29).

Theodore Roosevelt's veteran status, his ideology of manhood, and his articulation of American national identity linked the century's initial masculine ideal to a healthful, secure state and convinced Americans of World War I's positive value. Because, as Chauncey contends, "the Spanish-American War of 1898 and the spirit of militarism it engendered were widely celebrated as the savior of American manhood" (113), many looked to the United States' involvement in World War I as a stay against the degeneration of American manhood. Although the United States hesitated to enter the conflict, American men bent on proving their manhood met the eventual declaration of war with enthusiastic enlistment (Messner 9). For them World War I constituted a golden opportunity, and early twentieth-century definitions of heroic masculinity were formulated. Joe Dubbert says that "male heroes were portrayed as rugged individualists, self-reliant to the core, unflinchingly brave and courageous" (64). Such conceptions of heroic masculinity persist to the present day.

Since *Male Armor* contends that late twentieth-century representations of war continually resist or negate the traditional definitions of masculinity at stake in these early twentieth-century debates, its analyses center upon ways that war disrupts men's access to masculinity. As its title suggests, *Male Armor* explores the myriad ways men in contemporary U.S. culture have fortified their bodily, emotional, and mental protection, how they have attempted to apply to themselves and keep intact cultural definitions of masculinity or manhood. When men fail to exhibit actions commonly associated with masculinity as traditionally defined, they transgress, moving closer to the elements in gendered binaries describing what men are not. "Anyone who is unwilling or unable to become a soldier," Christian Appy remarks, "is simply a crybaby, a coward, and a fairy" (91).

The many ways this transgression from masculine to feminine, from dominant to abject, may occur constitute what I'll call the "special topics" of *Male Armor*'s investigations, the primary nodes under which the texts register successful or functional masculinity and that inform the readings the chapters forward. These include homosexuality, race, cowardice, bodily coherence, and sexual or heroic performance. Of these, homoeroticism and its attendant threat of homosexuality will inform the bulk of readings of novels of World War II, because at the time homosexuality likely registered as the most readily recognizable and most abhorrent threat to masculine function. The specter of homosexuality lingered throughout the remainder of the century because, as Patrick Hopkins concludes, "homosexuality's threat to masculinity . . . translates into a threat to what constitutes a man's sense of self" (112–13). While this threat appears to have abated slightly, as cultural understanding of gender developed and shifted over the latter half of the twentieth century, other challenges to hegemonic white masculinity emerged, particularly race, since the Vietnam War was the first conflict to field racially integrated troops. Christopher Looby, writing about the use of all-black regiments in the Revolutionary War, says that "to admit black men into the army would be to concede them the status of men, to grant their manhood by virtue of their admissibility to the male homosocial institution that had the most direct indicative relation to male identity of all institutions" (72). Compelling as it is for its account of the introduction of black soldiers into U.S. military history, Looby's argument registers as equally compelling for its implications regarding the integration of the armed services, because integration putatively placed black soldiers on the same footing as their white compeers and effectively disrupted the white/black binary undergirding hegemonic white dominance.

The other special topics of analysis here—cowardice, bodily coherence, and sexual or heroic performance—exist in complicated interrelations with issues such as sexuality and race but nevertheless serve important individual functions in defining soldierly masculinity. It is not, however, always possible to isolate one element from another in its critique of gender. As Judith Butler argues, "Because gender is not always constituted coherently or consistently in different historical contexts, and because gender intersects with racial, class, ethnic, sexual, and regional modalities of discursively constituted identities . . . it becomes impossible to separate out 'gender' from the political and cultural intersections in which it is invariably produced and maintained" (*Gender* 3). Because of these interdependencies, one special topic often registers as or metaphorizes another, such as homoerotic desire being experienced by a soldier as an impairment to his anatomical function and thus to his soldierly performance. Each element both informs and expresses expectations about masculinity, such that one stands in for the others and vice versa.

The textual analyses in *Male Armor* examine these special topics; identify influences on cultural perceptions of masculinity at the time of the texts' authoring; and highlight reactions, both soldierly and civilian, to those perceptions. These cultural contingencies, ranging from ideas discussed by psychologists, to images presented in film and advertising, to lyrics of popular songs, serve as barometers of the culture's understanding of manhood. History serves as an organizing convenience for the study, a scaffold supporting an elucidation of the persistent gap. Thus, the historical survey of cultural productions about war exists to manifest that though wars, times, and definitions of gender change, the gap between civilian expectation and soldierly experience persists. The texts studied here dramatize individual attempts to align cultural perceptions with the soldierly experience of war. So continual are such authorial attempts to reconcile perspectives that one could argue that they both begin to define a genre of representing war and yet recognize no generic boundary—the texts *Male Armor* samples vary among novels, plays, memoirs, film, and other popular forms like music, Web blogs, advertising, and general-readership magazines. In my reading such texts isolate the various challenges to wartime male "function" outlined above—homosexuality, race, cowardice, bodily coherence, sexual or heroic performance—as indicative of broader cultural definitions of masculinity. Furthermore, these texts demonstrate that soldiers feel they achieve successful masculinity (as measured by appropriate "function") tenuously or only temporally, instead of as a given identity. The study thus illuminates the illogic of American culture's investment in war as guarantor of traditional masculinity, because war more often unmakes than makes the man. From these conclusions the study derives its suggestion that a discontinuation of notions of heroic masculinity in the public at large comprises a potential avenue for dismantling the allure of the war enterprise.

## Dismantling the Tradition

The war novels analyzed in chapter 1, many written well after the end of the conflict, attempt to reconcile soldierly experience of the war with the radically different civilian conception of the conflict as just and demonstrative of American moral rectitude. Chapter 1's title, "'The Great General Was a Has-Been,'" references President Harry S. Truman's firing of General Douglas MacArthur in 1952 and the concomitant passing of World War II's image of heroic masculinity with the commencement of the Korean War. For many veterans of World War II, MacArthur's dismissal was tantamount to the enervation of their contribution, a dismissal they also experienced in societal demands for their conformity to the strictures of consumer culture and G.I. Bill education emergent after the war. Literary depictions of World War II often use postwar conformist culture as a foil and can be seen as participating in other 1950s cultural trends, like bachelor culture and motorcycle gangs, that are seemingly nostalgic for wartime's world of men without women or for outmoded examples of male heroic function. Chapter 1 explores veterans' reluctance to submit to a culture that emerged as increasingly emasculating of men; texts often feature men reenacting or reimagining soldierly masculinity. Such responses emerged well into the Korean and Cold War eras, with the publication of James Jones's *The Thin Red Line* (1962). Chapter 1 argues that novels like Jones's, as well as Norman Mailer's *The Naked and the Dead* (1948), Gore Vidal's *The City and the Pillar* (1952), and James Barr's *Quatrefoil* (1952), can be read as veterans' attempts to improve civilian understanding of World War II and the relationship between men and war, an understanding kept critically limited by the Office of War Information's control over the images and information to which the public was privy. The differences between civilians' and veterans' understanding, as portrayed in these novels, persisted into later twentieth-century war eras.

Chapter 2, "The Bridge to Vietnam," reads Joseph Heller's 1961 novel, *Catch-22*, as a historical bridge linking World War II, the novel's subject, with the Korean War, which it references, and the Vietnam War, which it eerily foresees.[5] The chapter analyzes Yossarian's character, under the general heading "AWOL masculinity," as a means of justifying the image of heroic masculinity Heller asks his audiences to accept. Because this image doesn't jibe with civilian expectations of soldierly service, this bridge also extends *Male Armor*'s investigation of the gap between civilian comprehension of war and the soldier's experience of it. The chapter discusses how the image of AWOL masculinity, and other images of the war enterprise featured in the novel, later became stock descriptions in war narratives of Vietnam and later wars.

During the Vietnam conflict the threat of the body in pieces metaphorically came to represent societal conceptions of successful male function, as sought by the soldiers who experienced the war. Chapter 3, "Envelope, Please," analyzes the use of body counts to replace reports of gains in territory as a means of gauging war progress and the resultant tug-of-war for soldiers between self-preservation and collective investment in the Vietnam conflict. The idea that any part of the enemy's body counted as a casualty added "the intact body" to the list of necessary attributes for masculine function, while twelve- to thirteen-month tours of duty and the first-time use of fully integrated ground troops increased the demands for unit cohesion, necessitating that difference be subsumed for the sake of the masculine collective and the prospects of the nation. The inside/outside binary for this collective aligns too neatly, in Michael Herr's *Dispatches* and David Rabe's *Streamers,* with the familiar masculine/feminine binary and is further complicated by the first-time introduction of African American soldiers into fully integrated combat units. In Herr's and Rabe's texts anything short of an intact bodily "envelope," whether individual or collective, threatens masculinity. Herr unwittingly feminizes all those "outside" the collective, including himself and all the black soldiers in his memoir, while Rabe's play places white and black, straight and gay soldiers into a cauldron that roils as they prepare to depart for Vietnam. Herr's eventual inability to enter the "masculine collective," and the death of Rabe's all-American boy at the hands of those outside traditional definitions of masculinity, signal the impossibility of subsuming difference and thus appear to reinforce the supremacy of traditional masculinity as white, hypermale, and soldierly—a supremacy that is culturally enforced. But given all the potential for injury in Vietnam, both texts finally reduce a man's achievement of manhood, his entry into the collective, to his ability to remain unimpaired. Thus, literature about the Vietnam conflict, largely influenced by public disapproval of the war, depicts the demand that the soldier privilege individual bodily coherence over traditional heroic function and consequently both challenges the societal perception and highlights the disparity between civilian belief and soldierly experience.

By the last decade of the twentieth century, postfeminist changes in definitions of masculinity had fully imbued American culture, yet expectations of traditional soldierly masculinity continued to inflect cultural representations of America's first Persian Gulf war. Chapter 4, "Winning This Time," argues that texts treating Operation Desert Storm, including David O. Russell's film *Three Kings* (1999) and Anthony Swofford's *Jarhead* (2003), redirected the cultural disinvestment in the notion of heroic masculinity wrought by Vietnam onto the expectation for a casualty-free war that would vitiate negative attitudes about the Vietnam conflict and effectively renarrativize the earlier war. In *Three Kings* the soldiers resist military authority for personal gain and attain a modified heroic status by devoting themselves to rescuing "the other" (typically read as feminine; here depicted as Arab). The three kings (or four, as the case may be) thus highlight American beneficence by disconnecting it from military venture, a narrative, the chapter argues, made popular in representations of the Vietnam War. *Jarhead,* on the other hand, charts Anthony Swofford's familial and personal compulsions to military service, which result in disillusionment during the First Gulf War and fervent regret afterward. Although their essentially traitorous behavior marks the soldiers in *Three Kings* and *Jarhead* as heroes within their respective texts, their behavior, as in all previously examined portrayals of men in war, does not coincide with civilian conceptions of heroic masculinity, though the culture shows no signs of altering its expectations of soldiers. *Jarhead*'s awkward shift to an antiwar stance (a shift ignored in Sam Mendes's November 2005 film version of the book) especially highlights the disparity between civilian belief in war's man-making status and the lived experience of war.[6] These two texts show how conceiving of Operation Desert Storm as a corrective to Vietnam in the American imagination merely scripts the former conflict onto the latter, failures and all, and problematizes the historicization of the First Gulf War.

*Male Armor* concludes with "Time Warp," a brief survey of early representations of the United States' Operation Iraqi Freedom: Nathaniel Fick's *One Bullet Away: The Making of a Marine Officer* and Jason Christopher Hartley's *Just Another Soldier: A Year on the Ground in Iraq.* The conclusion examines the relationship between reemergent cultural perceptions of traditional soldierly masculinity (energized by a militarist culture after September 11) and the experiences of combat soldiers cognizant of and influenced by those perceptions. From the eagerness, following September 11, to accord "hero" status to any person in public police, fire, or emergency service by dint of his/her employ, or to any individual willing and able to donate blood, to the ready regression to a "with us or against us" public rhetoric in light of the terrorist attacks, America's twenty-first century seems poised to rouse and reinvigorate traditional heroic masculinity and to urge Americans to war, much like Teddy Roosevelt did a century ago. While both Fick's and Hartley's works depict young men urged to patriotic displays of heroic masculinity, indeed convinced of war's ability to make them the men they envisioned, both also feature soldiers keenly aware of the bifurcation between their soldierly performance and their perceptions of themselves as men. Fick's and Hartley's fervent belief in war's man-making capacity emerges as chillingly problematic, especially as their disillusionment with the military enterprise colors their attempts to make sense of war afterward. Both authors willingly engage national justifications for war and deflect notions of gender onto traditional cultural definitions of war. Both texts thus suggest the continued reticence to critique the cultural equation of manhood with war. Like previous chapters of *Male Armor,* then, "Time Warp" interrogates whether theoretical understandings of gender blunt or ameliorate cultural appeals to heroic masculinity. In so doing, the conclusion realizes *Male Armor*'s central purposes: outlining the terms of masculinity to which the culture has ascribed and derailing contemporary America's continued use of appeals to soldierly masculinity to maintain a tacit, unquestioning justification for war as a national pastime.

## The Terrain of Men and War

As these chapter summaries indicate, *Male Armor*'s project forms a confluence of studies about war and about men, so it seems appropriate to identify this work's relationship to scholarship about war literature and gender—to introduce the terrain, as it were, that I hope to negotiate, coalesce, and enhance. When writing about war literature in the United States, one invariably encounters what Margot Norris terms "the impossibility of encompassing such a large field" (5), so, to some degree, every attempt to limit exposes an oversight. I am well aware that, as Alex Vernon concedes about his own text selection in *Soldiers Once and Still,* my choices will vex some readers. Since *Male Armor*'s central critical aim is to elucidate the function of a persistent gap between civilian expectations of war and a soldier's experience of it, the study focuses upon the texts best suited to manifest its claims. This is not to say, however, that the selected texts are the only ones that represent this persistent gap. In fact, as I'll explain presently, the mode of analysis undertaken in *Male Armor* constitutes a possible methodology for reading other textual representations of war, one perhaps both broadly applicable and definitional of the genre.

Additionally, my choice of terminology to refer collectively to the texts *Male Armor* studies may strike some as either needlessly vague or over-weeningly broad. I generally refer to the texts included for analysis as either "the texts *Male Armor* studies" or "representations of war." The former use generally implies my desire to not extend my analysis universally beyond the parameters of the study, whereas the latter signals my belief that such extensions are possible, if not desirable. In each case, however, the categori-zation is meant to make more specific the labels it appears to replace, such as "war literature." Because *Male Armor* does study film, and because some of the works included will likely not bear literary scrutiny, "war texts" and "representations of war" seem more appropriate labels than "war literature." Additionally, the terms "texts" and "representations" allow me to reference simultaneously the many genres included in the study, such as prose fiction, the nonfiction memoir, and drama.

To begin to narrow the focus of the study, I elected to examine contem-porary American culture, roughly defined as beginning at the end of World War II, but as indicated above, the link between masculinity and war in the American imaginary is time-honored. As a further delineation *Male Armor* focuses solely on texts written by men, because part of the func-tion of masculinity that the text explores involves men's experience of man-hood, and all of *Male Armor*'s texts self-consciously connect the author's or the characters' attitudes about war with ideas about manhood or masculine function. This focus is not meant to suggest that only men can write about masculinity, to privilege men's particular portrayals of their own lives and experiences, or to reify masculinist ideals. A study of women's writing in the field would provide interesting counterpoints to the observations presented here, but incorporating women's writing into the present study would have immensely widened its scope and perhaps transformed its discoveries. It's my hope, however, that the method of analysis employed in *Male Armor* could be used to launch such comparative work.

Of the many male-authored war texts available, all of the ones examined here were written by men with veteran status, the exceptions being Michael Herr, author of *Dispatches,* who spent two years in Vietnam as a correspondent, and David O. Russell, writer and director of *Three Kings*. Among the veteran authors service status varies, so all cannot be assumed to have had direct combat experience. All of them, however, have somewhat of an insider's status.[7] I don't mean to privilege these views or establish them as the only legitimate voices in representations of war. Rather, I selected them as a means of keeping the focus of study narrow.

Another and perhaps more controversial form of narrowing emerges in my decision to analyze only texts written by *white* male authors. This choice materialized as a result of my desire to explore what Michael Messner describes as "hegemonic masculinity[:] the form of masculinity that is dominant, [that] expresses (for the moment) a successful strategy for the domination of women, and . . . is also constructed in relation to various marginalized and subordinated masculinities (e.g. gay, black, and working-class masculinities)" (7–8). I see this exploration as decidedly feminist and committed to feminist ideals of equalizing power structures in culture. In Messner's formulation white masculinity emerges as the form against which all other forms of masculinity, and everything feminine or not masculine, are articulated. Significant scholarship already establishes that hegemonic masculinity denies these "other" forms of power, subjectivity, and self-realization as a means of maintaining its dominance, yet little work has focused explicitly on white masculinity to prove that it too is constructed and performed and must therefore have no real or natural existence to warrant or justify its domination.[8]

In fact, some recent gender theory has labeled white masculinity unassailable, and this too-ready acquiescence to the impenetrability of white male privilege is very much at stake in *Male Armor*'s analyses. Studies claiming unassailable white male hegemony consequently reemphasize white masculinity as the norm and effectively dismantle the theoretical work of gender theorists since the second wave of feminism. For instance, in her groundbreaking and necessary work *Female Masculinity*, Judith Halberstam concedes that "the structure of white male masculinity . . . seems impervious to criticism or attack and maintains hegemonic sway despite all challenges to its power" (275). Finding it "hard to be very concerned about the burden of masculinity on males" (273), Halberstam elects to "[turn] a blind eye to conventional masculinities and [refuses] to engage" (9). In a study that seems otherwise very concerned "not simply to create another binary in which masculinity always signifies power" (29), *Female Masculinity* unwittingly posits white male masculinity as the standard against which all alternate masculinities emerge, the norm that need not be performed, that just is. The texts studied in *Male Armor* propose just the opposite—that white men too struggle to define and/or attain their sense of a masculine or male self, their manhood. And while Halberstam questions whether "the non-performance is part of what defines white male masculinity" (235), by "refusing to engage" the *possibility* of white male performance of masculinity, her study effectively reifies the norm as nonperformative and enervates Judith Butler's seminal discovery that "if gender is something that one becomes—but can never be—then gender is itself a kind of becoming or activity." Gender, Butler continues, "ought not to be conceived as a noun or a substantial thing or a static cultural marker, but rather as an incessant and repeated action of some sort" (112).

Cursory examination of war representations produces numerous examples of white men who do not experience their manhood as always already extant. In fact, many such men go to war or conceive of soldiering as a means to embody cultural expectations about masculinity—in other words, as a way to perform masculinity. They come to war believing they will there locate and don a sense of maleness, power, and privilege that the culture has largely conditioned them to believe they will find but that, finally, they do not. *Male Armor* explores these experiences not to replicate studies that Halberstam claims "detail the fragilities of male socialization, the pains of manhood, the fear of female empowerment," though some catalogs of these undoubtedly occur, but to lay the groundwork for "taking apart the patriarchal bonds between white maleness and privilege" that Halberstam encourages (19). Laying this groundwork demands that *Male Armor* address works by white men directly. In so doing, *Male Armor* argues that even white males, though they may not conceptualize gender as performance, nevertheless behave in ways indicative of their belief that acts constitute manhood, that there's no *is* even to white masculinity. As David Savran argues, "masculinity is never possessed by the male subject . . . but is always pretended to" (178). *Male Armor* suggests that this holds true even for white men. They thus seem to have come to Wallace Stevens's "final belief" concerning their masculinity—the belief in a fiction.[9] The question is whether or not the fiction is a necessary one.

Does *Male Armor* hope to evoke pity for these men? Yes, somewhat, for they are surely the cogs in machines built by others, and indices of race and class contribute to their enlistment. Certainly they often make the supreme sacrifice. This pity is not meant, however, only to solidify their place as having been wronged or victimized by war, though this too certainly occurs. Instead the study hopes to reveal that white men do perform acts they link to gender and to suggest that one avenue for subverting patriarchal domination might be to convince American culture to replace external appearances, mannerisms, functions, and acts of traditional masculinity with internal values amenable to peaceful, productive manhood: values of nonviolent, positive support and care; of steadfastness in diplomacy and stubborn commitment to understanding cultures, peoples, and ideas foreign to one's own, so that no individual goes to war uncertain of what will be found there. It hopes, really, that no one goes to war at all.

## Lofty Ambitions

**In the end, none of us knows the correct direction or doctrine**
**that will end war, equalize gender, or unlink war from gender.**
—Joshua Goldstein, *War and Gender*

Recognizing the lacuna Joshua Goldstein notes in his substantive, interdisciplinary study, *War and Gender: How Gender Shapes the War System*, *Male Armor* proffers a "direction or doctrine" that aims to "unlink war from gender," just as 10,000 Maniacs, cited above, have done. Goldstein suggests that historians, social scientists, and other scholars of gender and war begin to think about the relationship between war and gender as a "feedback loop," in which "the war system influences the socialization of children into all their gender roles." These roles, Goldstein asserts, then buttress the system they create and support (410–11). After examining numerous possible "causes" for the gendering of war as male, from chromosomal to hormonal, from physical to psychological, Goldstein locates the feedback loop he describes as the most likely and most relevant area of critique for theorists hoping to accomplish the end of war. Likewise, in his overtly literary study *Soldiers Once and Still*, Alex Vernon encourages the examination of war literature in a cultural context and suggests that "if readers cannot afford to lose touch with the human element in the text, neither can we afford to lose touch with the cultural dimension—the dimension that frequently sends soldiers to war in the first place and that plays into their postwar perceptions of their wars and consequently of themselves" (39). In the exchange between culture and the war experience, Vernon indicates, texts often emerge as mediations that vividly portray the functioning loop—they both reflect and influence the public's perception of the veteran's experience of war.

The interrogations *Male Armor* undertakes reveal the outlines of the masculinity/war loop in contemporary America and constitute nascent work in directions suggested by Goldstein and Vernon. While the aspects of the loop and the relative influence of various ideas about masculinity and/or war vary over the period of the study, the tension of mutual reinforcement among the elements persists despite alterations to theoretical understandings of gender and changes wrought by the gradual introduction of women into the U.S. Armed Forces. In light of current U.S. policy of preemptive invasion, and of the general postmillennial reevaluation of the effects of feminism and queer theory on gender equality, *Male Armor* provides a pressingly necessary interrogation of both the attitudes that facilitate any public approval of the preemptive doctrine and the shortcomings of theoretical understandings of gender that have allowed for continued investment in war as a man-making and nation-building enterprise.

If *Male Armor* succeeds in making visible the persistent gap between civilian expectation and soldierly experience of war, it thus proffers several critical contributions to the fields of literary and gender studies. First, readers will learn that civilian America has consistently imposed standards of male performance upon soldiers that the soldiers have difficulty upholding. These standards inform soldiers' reticence about their war experiences and subtend difficulties soldiers have in reintegrating to civilian society. Queer theorists and scholars of gender will gain credible demonstration that no aspect of masculinity, including hitherto hegemonic white masculinity, can be said to be equitably distributed, entrenched, and unassailable. And for those who study representations of war, the persistent gap *Male Armor* elucidates provides a methodology for analyzing war texts and for understanding how they function for the public at large, the role they attempt to fill. I see this methodology as broadly applicable, pertinent to texts written by women and texts composed long after the war periods they adumbrate. Among such possibilities, but beyond the parameters of the present study, I'd include Pat Barker's World War I trilogy, Leslie Marmon Silko's *Ceremony,* Joan Didion's *Democracy,* and Jayne Anne Phillips's *Machine Dreams.* Study of such texts using the methodology *Male Armor* proposes might even help scholars begin to define the genre of war literature, as the presence of the gap could be seen to correspond to the generic distinction. With thorough-going critical attention to such outlying vectors, perhaps scholars can at last enunciate the "direction or doctrine" that will finally end war, and it is this most important work that critics must commence.

# CHAPTER 1

# "THE GREAT GENERAL WAS A HAS-BEEN"

*The World War II Hero in
1950s Conformist Culture*

## Ernest Hemingway, General Douglas MacArthur, and the Enervation of America's War Heroes

In his 1952 novella, *The Old Man and the Sea,* Ernest Hemingway introduced his American reading audience to the term *salao,* which means the "worst form of unlucky" (9). Hemingway attributes the term to his protagonist, Santiago, and describes him as "thin and gaunt with deep wrinkles in the back of his neck" (9). "Many of the fisherman" who reside in Santiago's village "made fun" of him, but "he was not angry" (11). Santiago and Manolin, the village boy who befriends him, construct fictions to ease their daily labor for food. They talk of a net they no longer own, of a pot of yellow rice and fish they do not have to eat, and of American baseball games they will never see. When alone, Santiago occupies his time dreaming of Africa "and the long golden beaches and the white beaches, so white they hurt your eyes," that he visited as a boy and where now, in dreams, "he lived . . . every night" (24). Santiago also recalls his day-long wrestling match, which "started on a Sunday morning and ended on a Monday morning" (70). He triumphed, and "for a long time after that everyone had called him The Champion" (70). But despite Santiago's pride in these reminiscences, the preeminent personality trait Hemingway grants Santiago is humility: "He was too simple to wonder when he had attained humility. But he knew he had attained it and he knew it was not disgraceful and it carried no loss of true pride" (13–14). Santiago counterbalances the physical effects of age, which threaten to steal away his livelihood, with mental comfort in recollections of his past and faith in his "many tricks" and "resolution" (23).

The novella depicts in detail Santiago's solitary fishing venture on his eighty-fifth day without a catch. Not long after setting out, the old man hooks the largest fish of his career and spends nearly two days trying to overcome its amazing strength. The duel becomes more a test of will and endurance than of skill, and as Santiago battles the giant fish, the reader revisits ideas about what makes a man, long established in Hemingway's corpus and publicly associated with the author himself. Santiago thinks, "Pain does not matter to a man" (84). He is grateful that he "know[s] how to suffer like a man" (92). Eventually, Santiago conquers the will of his fish, kills it, and lashes it to the side of his small boat. A Hemingway hero once again appears to triumph on the hunt, until sharks besiege Santiago's craft. Santiago musters every ounce of strength at his disposal and improvises every weapon he can in order to stave off the frenzy, but he returns to port with nothing but a skeleton as testament to his achievement. But the skeleton proves inadequate to garnering Santiago the valorization that Hemingway masculinity requires, as only Manolin talks to Santiago once he returns.[1] All appears to be lost for this hero, who becomes dependent upon the boy. Manolin brings the old man food he begs off local villagers and encourages Santiago to rest and recover. Manolin insists that "there is much that [he] can learn" (126) from Santiago. So the old man falls asleep to dream of lions in Africa, knowing he still has uses, even though he is *salao*.

*The Old Man and the Sea* was an instant success, pleasing readers and critics alike, garnering Hemingway the Pulitzer Prize, and securing for him, in the minds of many, the Nobel Prize in Literature. After a series of rather dismal, unsuccessful novels, it appeared that Papa was back on top of his game.[2] But the din of the encomiums obscured some of the realities of a text that clearly expresses not only its author's fears of his own uselessness but a startling redefinition of the hero and the notions of manliness hitherto identified with Hemingway. Santiago is an old man, no longer good at his craft, his tricks and resolution nullified by his aging and by forces of nature he cannot control. Moreover, the old man realizes his uselessness, accepts it with humility, and founders in memories of childhood places far away. Santiago's *salao* image and his dependence upon Manolin must have resonated incongruously with the Hemingway man as the American public had come to perceive him, but the public loved the hero anyway. So why was the book so admired? Why did critics and readers laud the "return" of Papa Hemingway?

This chapter explores the curious nature of 1950s public adulation of anachronistic models of masculinity, such as that Hemingway experienced with Santiago, and explains that admiration in terms of altering perceptions of successful manhood following World War II. It registers the locus of the disjunction between civilian ideals of heroic manhood and authorial presentation of alternative masculinities in governmental manipulation of public knowledge during World War II. The following analyses of World War II novels by Norman Mailer, James Jones, Gore Vidal, and James Barr reveal that these veteran-novelists present their images of masculinity as both a corrective to civilian disinformation and an anodyne to the rise of conformist masculinity in 1950s domestic consumer society. These novels, as I read them, force a reimagination of masculinity through either the specter of homoerotic desire or the presentation of homosexual identity, all within a military environment—hence the novels' use of a World War II setting. The emergence of the feminine signified by homoerotic desire or homosexuality seems surprising as an alternative to masculinity, but this must be understood as the most readily recognizable spoiler of masculinity for a civilian public uncertain of precisely how to define manhood. As the novels attempt to reimagine masculinity via the suppressed form of the male/female binary, they simultaneously suggest that the public's understanding of war is incomplete, ill informed, or off base. Thus, the following examination of masculinity in several World War II novels delineates *Male Armor*'s theme of the persistent gap between civilian understanding and soldierly experience of war.

Perhaps Hemingway's cognizance of civilian disinformation about war informed his presentation of Santiago, as his literary career featured numerous examples of his attempt to rectify the gap between civilian understanding and soldierly experience.[3] The fisherman's stoic acceptance of his fate, and his inability to attract accolades for his deed, certainly aren't unusual results in a Hemingway novel. That the public would laud them nonetheless prompts Hemingway biographer Kenneth Lynn to comment that "people give up on their heroes reluctantly" (566). In reassessing *The Old Man and the Sea,* Lynn asserts that "today there is only one question worth asking about The Old Man." Specifically, "how could a book that lapses repeatedly into lachrymose sentimentality and is relentlessly pseudo-Biblical, that mixes cute talk about baseball with crucifixion symbolism of the most appalling crudity, have evoked such a storm of applause from highbrows and middlebrows alike—and in such overwhelming numbers?" (566). Clearly, Lynn locates the success of *The Old Man and the Sea* in the public's confusion between Ernest Hemingway's persona and his work, the latter signifying less in face of the former.[4] What the public and critics refused to see was that the persona had changed as well.

Lynn places this transformation of the Hemingway hero within a set of specific historical events and attitudes that both influence and undergird the arguments proffered in this chapter. Post–World War II America's introduction to Cold War exigencies coincided, according to Lynn, with the "nation's vanished sense of illimitable power" (566), for although the United States was in possession of the most powerful weaponry known to mankind, use of that power offered mass extinction as its purchase. Moreover, a nation on constant guard against the ills of Communism, which threatened to overrun world governments and pervade the fibers of American society, could never be a nation confidently at ease with its status as a world power. The Cold War presented Americans with something they had not experienced since the Civil War: an enemy lodged on their own soil, perhaps in the hearts and minds of their neighbors.

This newly perceived threat enervated the heroes of America's past, for constraining it demanded approaches previously unimagined. Old rules no longer applied. Never was this so clearly brought to the attention of Americans than when President Harry Truman fired America's great World War II general Douglas MacArthur during the Korean War. After his victory at the battle of Inchon, MacArthur had attempted to carry on the traditional military strategy of attack and subdue. Truman, however, feared that the full-frontal push suggested by MacArthur might lead to a nuclear rebuff by the Communists and commanded MacArthur not to execute such a push. When the general protested, he was promptly fired. In the nuclear age, Truman's actions suggested, military business was no longer business as usual; a compromising diplomacy would have to replace brute displays of force. MacArthur's return to the United States was heralded as the coming home of a great war hero, but, as Lynn claims, "the citizens who cheered him on curbsides in 1951 and who named boulevards, causeways, and high schools in his honor knew that he stood for an outdated philosophy of international conduct. The great general was a has-been" (568). So too was Hemingway's Santiago, who like MacArthur was lauded by a reading public that ought to have known better.

The change in America's military policies evidenced by the dismissal of MacArthur heralded an epistemological crisis in American minds, for the removal of America's heroes necessitated reassessments of what victory meant both for individual men and for the United States as a nation. Lynn summarizes these attitudes and attempts to explain them: "The American hero was perceived to have changed. Somehow he had lost something. . . . It wasn't his prowess. It wasn't his resourcefulness. And by and large it wasn't his belief in himself, although the pangs of self-doubt were not unfamiliar to him. . . . There was no longer any common agreement about what the meaning of winning was, so that no victory ever brought unalloyed satisfaction" (568).

To the historical observer the radical nature of the definitional changes Lynn recounts, as well as the misgivings they prompted, may be difficult to perceive, but the stories of MacArthur and of Hemingway's Old Man presage at least some of the alteration American ideals were undergoing. A generation earlier, Americans had entered World War I convinced of the notion that whatever forces threatened American notions of masculinity, and hence of heroism, could be thwarted by participation in a war. America's victory in World War I assuaged masculine doubts until the arrival of the Depression, which sufficed to unman many Americans. But heady optimism, coupled with governmental propaganda, once again triumphed as the United States entered World War II with the expectation of victory and of the resultant renewal of masculinity, via soldierly and economic invigoration. When that victory was achieved late in 1945, expectations of the primacy of the American man *should* have been realized. Susan Faludi catalogs these expectations in *Stiffed,* her study of men who came of age in the baby-boom generation. Faludi states that "the United States came out of World War II with a sense of itself as a masculine nation, our 'boys' ready to assume the mantle of national authority and international leadership. The nation claimed an ascendancy over the world, men an ascendancy over the nation, and a male persona of a certain type ascendancy over men" (16). Everything, in other words, that Americans believed about the war effort and the changes it had wrought at home convinced American men that the world was their oyster.

But the promise Faludi summarizes also contained the seeds of what would become male revolt in the 1950s, replacing, and thus glossing, individual experience with a national narrative. The idea that returning veterans were "our boys," owned by a nation that would speak for them, created a distinction between the civilian view of the men and the perspective of the men themselves. Veterans' perspectives would only become part of the American experience of World War II once these men began to recount their experiences, and the stories they told differed from civilian belief. After the parades ended, veterans encountered not ascendancy, but a confining expectation of domestic manhood that contradicted the masculinist military values they had gone to the war to uphold. MacArthur's replacement and Santiago's superfluity were also theirs. David Buchbinder recounts veterans' reaction to transformations in civilian society: "The men . . . feared that their strengths and skills as men might no longer be required; that, indeed, they had been emasculated by the very practice—war—which had traditionally allowed men to display masculine qualities such as courage, fortitude, endurance, stoicism and sheer physical strength" (8). Hemingway's Santiago claims these attributes for himself. The narrative, however, disallows him the benefit of possessing them, and what may be perceived as a metaphor for the author can be construed for returning veterans as well. The prewar optimism over American masculine regeneration was betrayed postwar by the knowledge that victory had wrought yet another, more insidious war. This knowledge sufficed to countermand the previous notion that war produced men, replacing the promise of soldierly masculinity for veterans with misgivings about heroism, misgivings that would permeate stories written of the war.

The dissolution of formerly held notions of heroism and masculinity precipitated the formulation of new ideas about what it meant to be a man in America. Postwar prosperity turned American minds to the creation of new images of heroic behaviors and manliness consistent with economic growth. The American propaganda machine promulgated attitudes about what men would do and be in 1950s America, attitudes aimed directly at returning veterans finding it difficult to assimilate into postwar society. Advertising culture showed how soldiers could still benefit their country by contributing to its newfound prosperity and by submitting their individual wills to the larger project of societal growth and betterment. Hence, as Joe Dubbert argues, the notion of the 1950s conformist man was born and disseminated: "What came to be recognized as the 'normal social groove' after the war and in the fifties," Dubbert contends, "was the absorption of many individuals into very large organizations, business, industries, and colleges. Individuals were expected to accept the company line because the company, with all of its collective wisdom, really knew what was best. What followed was a further erosion of individualism and the establishment of a conforming and standardizing atmosphere" (242).

Coupled with the insistence that men conform to notions of public behavior through their social interrelations was the suggestion that men's private behaviors correspond to the veneer of conformity as well. As a result, the image of the breadwinner became the masculine ideal for the 1950s and the home his new kingdom. Rowena Chapman summarizes the civilian expectations that would ironically begin to define masculinity through the domestic sphere: "Men were encouraged to marry early (average age 23) and to take on the sole support of a wife and family. A whole panoply of professionals were enlisted to persuade men that the breadwinner ethic was the only state for an adult male, and that the achievement of maturity necessitated the successful completion of a number of 'life tasks' namely marriage and fatherhood. Failure to complete these tasks was incompatible with adult masculinity; those who failed were characterised as either not fully adult, or not fully masculine" (233).

In defining "adult masculinity" via the nuclear family and the domestic sphere, 1950s conformist culture completely reversed the late-Victorian fears of emasculation that World War I was supposed to assuage. Moreover, adherence to the ideal nuclear family buttressed prodigious economic growth because it also enlisted men in the acquisition of the numerous domestic gadgets that the revved-up war economy began to produce postwar. In his study of Cold War America, Robert J. Corber notes that "men were no longer encouraged to show initiative or to exert their independence from the domestic sphere. Rather, they were expected to define themselves through their identities as consumers" (5–6). Thus, new expectations of men were aligned with America's transition to postwar production and consumption of domestic goods, and these expectations were among those that contributed to veterans' difficulty in reintegrating into civilian society postwar.

But how could the civilian public have developed views of men's duties, desires, and functions that were so radically different from those the returning veterans held themselves?

I'd like to suggest that the nature of civilian America's experience of World War II enabled these diverging views of masculinity that, at most, veteran authors may have wished to amend and, at least, informs their portrayals of soldiers and the war. Civilian experience of World War II was predominantly shaped by the Office of War Information's iron-fisted control over images viewed by civilians. In his book *The Censored War,* George Roeder describes the policies adopted by the newly constructed Pentagon to maintain public support of the war's execution and management by limiting what the public saw. Roeder's central purpose in outlining this development parallels the investigation *Male Armor* makes into war literature: Roeder insists that a radical disjuncture between civilian visual experience and veteran combat experience permeated the postwar atmosphere, creating "the possibilities of misunderstandings" (123) that the present study locates in representations of war. Roeder traces the origin of this gap to what Americans were allowed to see throughout the duration of the war and to the attitudes such controls germinated, claiming that "during the war the U.S. government, with extensive support from other public and private organizations, made the most systematic and far-reaching effort in its history to shape the visual experience of the citizenry" (2). Roeder delineates some of these restrictions: government officials forbade "publication not only of photographs of those maimed in combat but also of pictures of racial conflicts on military bases, violent confrontations between G.I.s and their foreign allies, and other evidence of disunity within their own camp. They suppressed photographs of shell-shocked G.I.s, of those killed in jeep accidents, and of victims of Allied bombing raids and U.S. chemical warfare experiments" (3).

Additionally, the government censored any "photographs of American soldiers who died in training accidents, who shot themselves, and who were killed or wounded by 'friendly fire'" (24). Roeder further claims that "official images never showed soldiers crying" (24) and that, throughout the war, "military authorities remained alert for sexually ambivalent images" (49). He also cites "a rule maintained throughout the war" that "forbade publication of any photograph revealing identifiable features of the American dead" and asserts that "censors kept emotionally wounded Americans out of sight throughout the war" (16).

Images that the Office of War Information (OWI) did allow Americans to view were part of a massive propaganda campaign meant "to create reassuring visual comparisons of military and home front activities" (Roeder 59).[5] Americans were led to believe not only that soldiers were performing duties similar to those of civilians but that every action taken at home contributed to the overall well-being of the nation. But Roeder also notes that "even as the government flattered civilians with images comparing home front and combat activities, it told soldiers that what they were going through was different from anything stay-at-homes could imagine" (51)—in effect, further widening the gap. Whereas combat soldiers may have witnessed death firsthand daily, Roeder charts only a gradual increase in the violent content of the images civilians viewed over the entirety of the war and little that would suggest American soldiers suffered violent injury or death themselves. He relates that "during America's first year in the war only a few published photographs . . . acknowledged the costs of American involvement, such as one of a Marine in agony from wounds suffered at Guadalcanal" (10). "By September 1943," he continues, "concerns about public complacency led officials to release from this grim archive [the Pentagon's 'Chamber of Horrors'] photographs that showed death, but not yet bloody death" (1). This public complacency, "indicated by worker absenteeism, job switching, strikes and decreases in voluntary enlistments" (Roeder 15), was thought to be remediable through depictions of American soldiers making the ultimate sacrifice. But despite increasing images of American dead released to buffer civilian support, it was not until the "spring of 1945, amid celebrations marking the end of World War II in Europe," that "the blood of an American soldier was first shed on the pages of *Life* magazine" (Roeder 1).

Roeder also recounts how the Hollywood film industry contributed to the gap between the public perception of war and veterans' experience of it. Though less reticent to depict American dead than official government publications were, movies consistently idealized the manner of their dying: "Americans saw fictional counterparts of their country's soldiers die on the nation's seventeen thousand movie screens soon after Pearl Harbor, nearly two years before the release of photographs and newsreels of actual death. But in these early films American deaths, always portrayed as heroic and meaningful, never hinted at the capacity of the machinery of modern warfare to mutilate the human body" (Roeder 21).

Paul Fussell expresses a similar opinion about the nobility of death in these films and shows how, like the Office of War Information, Hollywood also gradually escalated the realism of its portrayals of death: "By [the 1944 release of *Thirty Seconds over Tokyo*] even a Hollywood film could go so far as to suggest that wounded men scream and cry and that men losing limbs experience severe shock, but as always there is a silver lining: at home salvation awaits, for their women will comfort them. In all these films . . . good triumphs, which means that the success story, Hollywood's dominant narrative model, was easily accommodated to the demands of wartime moral meaning" (*Wartime* 191). Even though the "success story" Fussell describes coincides with the United States' moral justification for participating in the war in the first place, the stories of individual veterans, especially those returning with debilitating wounds, could not be entirely contained within the success model.

In *Male Subjectivity at the Margins,* Kaja Silverman examines World War II films that attempt realistic depictions of soldiers returning to civilian life, and her analysis crystallizes the issues facing these returnees, principally changing notions of heroism and masculinity. Silverman claims that in films of the postwar era, "the 'hero' returns from World War II with a physical or psychic wound which marks him as somehow deficient, and which renders him incapable of functioning smoothly in civilian life" (53). Here Silverman argues that veterans experience any such incapacitation as castration or emasculation. By merely placing the word "hero" in quotation marks, she delineates the predicament of the wounded combat veteran: *hero* no longer signifies for the emasculated man. Thus, Silverman claims, the films "dramatize the vulnerability of conventional masculinity" (53). Roeder also recognizes this shift in signification when he writes that "the greatest problem facing many [combat veterans suffering debilitating wounds] would be not their physical condition but public reactions to it" (98).

But for the purpose of my argument here, perhaps the most interesting aspect of Silverman's analysis is her tracing of the critical response to the release of *The Best Years of Our Lives.* In order to add emotional depth to the portrayal of Homer, the double amputee depicted in the film, studio executives decided to cast an actual amputee veteran, Harold Russell, to play the role. Silverman relates that critic Robert Warshow's 1947 essay on the film faults the film for its casting and claims, in Silverman's words, "too much authenticity" and an unwitting elision of "the boundary between cinema and life" (72). Under most circumstances cinema would perhaps be lauded for its ability to so distinctly depict reality. In this instance, however, Warshow might as well have been speaking for a nation of civilians who feared this erasure of the difference between art and life. Government and private controls over the images Americans were allowed to see rendered civilians ill prepared for the veterans' return and created myriad "possibilities for misunderstanding" that writers would spend the next decade attempting to countenance and overcome.

## The Realist Novel: Homoerotic Masculinity

In *The Hearts of Men* Barbara Ehrenreich describes "a new kind of veteran" returning home from World War II, "whose memories of masculine adventure made them chafe at post-war civilian 'conformity'" (31). Many of them believed that "conformity destroys not only men's souls, but their very manhood" (Ehrenreich 31), and they resisted the new norms in newly emergent ways, including rebel culture as popularized by James Dean and male gangs, which led in turn to an increase in incidences of juvenile delinquency. These alternative forms of masculinity in 1950s America involved a retreat to the homosocial organization of military life as a means to counter the domesticated, consumerist ideal. Robert J. Corber observes that "men protested the rise of the 'organization man' by joining motorcycle and other types of gangs that contributed to the spread of 'juvenile delinquency,' which became a national obsession in the fifties. Such gangs allowed them to recover forms of male homosocial bonding that were actively discouraged because they conflicted with the Fordist organization of production and consumption" (9). These renegade concordances of men threatened domestic tranquility in their implicit preference for all-male over mixed company and for bachelor status over the nuclear family offered in the home or in the burgeoning suburbs.

I would like to suggest that civilian America's need for new heroes caused these postwar retaliatory activities and influenced men's regress to the military's all-male society—the postwar behaviors required of them did not match their learned expectations of masculinity, expectations that urged them to war. Once home and faced with the realization that the heroes Americans now sought had not been created by World War II, veterans of the war began to doubt the purpose of their involvement individually and that of the nation as a whole. If heroic notions of masculinity no longer obtained, they asked, why had they fought to prove their manhood and served a country that seemed unappreciative?

One facet of the novelistic presentation of World War II is evident in the milieu of these male homosocial regressions: realistic portrayals of the war appear to rescript civilian understanding of the conflict so that civilians might better apprehend the war experience and thus desist in demands for men's conformity. Both Norman Mailer's *The Naked and the Dead* (1948) and James Jones's *The Thin Red Line* (1961) invent hypothetical campaigns in the Pacific theater for the purpose of renarrating the war for their audiences. The writers of these novels perhaps believed that by portraying the war as realistically as possible, they could reinstate lost notions of masculinity. It stands to reason that, by demonstrating the brutality of the struggle that the rush to consumer culture threatened to efface, the authors hoped to alter new civilian expectations of domesticity. Whereas revered World War I novels, like Hemingway's *A Farewell to Arms* and John Dos Passos's *1919,* employ the war as subject matter and narrative setting, they shy away from depictions of combat itself. In the first major American novel to be published after World War II, *The Naked and the Dead,* Mailer describes combat activities directly. Praised for its realistic portrayals, Mailer's novel remains one of the most acclaimed novels to come out of the war.[6] Likewise, James Jones's *The Thin Red Line* also dramatizes battle sequences. In the space of little more than a generation, then, descriptions of combat had shifted from being unnecessary in the war novel to being integral to its completion. The returning American veterans' disillusionment with a postwar civilian society shielded from much of war's reality partially explains why this shift transpired and suggests the widening gap between civilians' and combat veterans' experiences of war in the middle of the twentieth century. While civilians had seen their at-home activities compared to those of the soldiers at war, soldiers in training had been instructed to believe that "stay-at-homes" were ignorant of war's realities, and this belief compounded their later disenchantment. When read in light of these opposing notions of the conflict, novels portraying realistic accounts of war appear to be participating in an attempt to rehistoricize it, to introduce civilians to stories of war they had not heard.

While the depiction Mailer offers never feigns a historic source (the setting is a fictional island in the Pacific, Anopopei, the campaign a product of Mailer's imagination), Mailer's portrayals of military hierarchy and battle experience nevertheless attempt realistic presentation. The novel follows the experience of I and R platoon on Anopopei in a campaign under the direction of Major General Edward Cummings. Over the course of the United States' defeat of Japanese general Toyaku and its seizure of the island, Mailer introduces the reader to the members of I and R through a series of "Time Machine" segments, which narrate details of each member's civilian life. In a manner that surely presages future military narratives, Mailer's I and R platoon microcosmically comes to reflect all of American society, with the exception of African American soldiers, whom the armed forces had not yet integrated. The I and R platoon contains single men and married men with children, career military men, enlisted men, and conscripted men. Some are young, others well into careers such as teaching. The educational achievements of the crew run the gamut, from little more than grade school to the completion of a college degree. Mailer also uses his characters to represent many of the major ethnic and religious groups in the United States. Martinez, the prized scout from San Antonio, accounts for Hispanic and Catholic America, while Lieutenant Wakara represents not only the Japanese American experience of the relocation camps, where his family resides, but also the voice of the Japanese army itself when he serves as translator for the journal found on a Japanese infantryman. Minetta is Italian, and Casimir "Polack" Czienwicz Polish. Recon, another name for I and R, also contains two Jews: still-practicing Joey Goldstein and Herman Roth, who proffers his belief that practitioners of Judaism cannot be viewed as a race. The characters also hail from geographically diverse parts of the United States: Red Valsen from a mining town in Montana; Woodrow Wilson from the South; and Gallagher, the voice of the text's most virulent anti-Semitic and homophobic remarks, from Boston.

To further accentuate the novel's realism, Mailer's characters undergo experiences that would later become, like their ethnic and religious divisions, stock for combat soldiers in war novels. Hennessey plays the role of the innocent boy killed in his first firefight. Minetta feigns madness in an attempt to earn a permanent reprieve from combat, while others contemplate wounding themselves in order to escape. While none of the soldiers in Recon receives a "Dear John" letter from his wife or girlfriend, some have their lovers stop writing to them, and Gallagher's wife dies during childbirth. As a group the soldiers collect "souvenirs," like samurai swords and gold teeth, from the dead Japanese. And although they ultimately win their battle, like the soldiers Hemingway portrayed after World War I, their victory is not glorious, the soldiers not characterized as heroes. They thus figure much like Harold Krebs, in Hemingway's "Soldier's Home," in their disillusionment.[7] But Mailer makes their disappointment immediate, rather than reflective, as their patrol proves unnecessary and the deaths of Hearn, Wilson, and Roth in vain.

*The Naked and the Dead* inherits some of its narrative details from Hemingway's and Dos Passos's World War I novels, and it refigures them in ways that later war novelists would model. Mailer's detailed accounts of the soldiers' cowardice and fear, for example, would figure increasingly in other World War II and later twentieth-century war writing. The pervasiveness of soldierly misgivings here prompts Andrew Gordon to remark that "every man in this novel, without exception, is unsure of his potency and terrified of being less than a man" (61). For example, Brown expresses his fear in a conversation with Martinez while Recon is out on patrol: "You know what scares me, Japbait? I'll tell ya, my nerves are gone. Sometimes I'm afraid I'll just go to pieces and I won't be able to do a goddam thing." Brown goes on to muse that he "had worried about this many times," but that "he gained some satisfaction in admitting it, excusing himself ahead of time so that the onus would be less if his failure was realized" (461).

When comparing Mailer's narrative with those of Hemingway, one realizes that notions of heroism were sustained after World War I by veterans' reticence in talking about fear and cowardice. In the seventh interchapter of *In Our Time*, for instance, a soldier experiencing fear during a bombardment prays emphatically to Jesus for rescue, promising to tell everyone of his survival through the grace of Christ (67). When the conflict is over, however, the soldier doesn't tell anyone because telling would entail the admission of fear and cowardice. Likewise, Krebs, in "A Soldier's Home," though he recognizes his cowardice during the war, refuses to share his realization with anyone in his family. His cowardice renders him impotent in the face of his mother's religion and of romantic involvement with the girls in his town, whom he watches "walking on the other side of the street" (*In Our Time* 72), his physical distance from them symbolic of his impotence in interrelation. However, Mailer's soldiers' willingness to confess to fear in combat and their constant battles with cowardice directly contradict the images of soldiers in combat that civilians had been allowed to see by the Office of War Information. Americans simply were not permitted to believe that soldiers might be afraid and that this fear might cause them to "crack up," when, as Roeder relates, the reality was that "on average an infantryman could 'last' about two hundred days before breaking down" (16).

The realistic picture Mailer paints of military life furthers the demarcation he creates between the soldierly and the civilian experience of the war, not only delineating the varied experiences of soldiers but also railing against conformist 1950s conceptions of masculinity. The military's all-male environs create the opportunity for the development of male-male affectional relations and for homosexual sex, both of which reject postwar images of masculine conformity. The possibility of homoerotic desire or homosexuality emerges in *The Naked and the Dead* in the relationship between General Cummings and Lieutenant Hearn, the general's assistant. Hearn's initial ambivalence toward the general is quickly replaced by more negative assessments of Cummings's character: "Before Hearn had come to the division he had heard nothing but praise for his [the general's] techniques . . . but Hearn had discovered quite early that he was a tyrant, a tyrant with a velvet voice, it is true, but undeniably a tyrant" (78). Because "like all men of great vanity, the General was looking for an intellectual equal" (78), one would expect Hearn to be flattered by the fact that "in the two weeks since they had landed [Hearn] had been in the General's tent talking with him almost every night" (78) and by the fact that "the General treated him as an equal" (83). Hearn, however, views their relationship as a competition in which he must prove himself, beyond the ways in which subordinate men attempt to impress their superiors, perhaps because "at the proper moment" the General "jerked him again from the end of a string, establish[ing] the fundamental relationship of general to lieutenant with an abrupt startling shock like the slap of a wet towel" (83).

Hearn's covertly sexual terms—the wet towel resonant of locker-room banter taking place in the nude—suggest the nature of Cummings's interest in Hearn, and perhaps vice versa. The imputation of homosexuality, and hence the possibility of threatened masculinity, exists for both characters in their respective "Time Machine" segments, as well as elsewhere in the text.

At one point in Hearn's "Time Machine" segment, Hearn tells a friend: "You know when nothing else is left I'm going to become a fairy, not a goddam little nance, you understand but a nice upright pillar of the community, live on green lawns. Bisexual. Never a dull moment, man or woman, it's all the same to you, exciting" (340). Hearn here reflects the combination of suburban conformity and sexual rebelliousness characteristic of bachelor culture. Additionally, while in college, Hearn "deserts the beach many afternoons, the Sally Tendeckers and her replacements, spends the nights writing short stories. . . . The changes come slowly at first, then quickly" (339). While on the surface Hearn's rejection of leisure and female companionship appears aimed at improving his intellect, his educational pursuits stereotypically implicate him in an entrance into homosexual society. He reads gay poets—Housman, Rilke, Blake, Stephen Spender. Like a stereotypical homosexual he writes and attends the ballet and the theater.

Homosexual implications also exist in General Cummings's "Time Machine" segment. One of the first images the reader encounters is of "Edward, age seven . . . sitting in a corner, sewing snips of thread into a scrap of cloth," because "Ma said it was okay" (405). His mother takes Edward on clandestine afternoon outings to paint the local country scenery, forcing him to promise he will not tell his father. The father, meanwhile, visits the town doctor about the boy. The doctor replies, "Well, now, Mr. Cummings, there ain't a damn thing can be done now, it's over my head, if he were a little older I'd say take the boy over to Sally's and let him git some jism in his system" (407). In Edward's military high school there are "the crushes of course," like the one he has on "the cadet colonel, a tall dark-haired youth" (408). Appearing to reach "normal" maturity, however, the future general marries, but after a year of reasonably good sexual relations with his wife, "it is completely naked, apparent to her, that he is alone, that he fights out battles with himself upon her body" (416). Given all the evidence, those battles would seem to be internal ones with his homoerotic desires.

With homosexual desire thus implied for both Cummings and Hearn, the culmination of their relationship plays out in two separate scenes in the general's tent. The first involves a game of chess that the general invites Hearn to play. At the invitation Hearn states, "If someone walks in, it'll be a pretty sight," to which the general replies, "Clandestine, eh?" (178). Ostensibly, the difference in their ranks constitutes any transgression to be remarked, but the implication that they are undertaking something secretive raises the bar slightly, because according to Hearn, the game "made everything between them more overt. There seemed something vaguely indecent about it" (178). Perhaps in the absence of their insinuated sexual attraction for one another, Hearn would not feel as he does. After the general defeats Hearn, their discussion of chess strategies turns into a conversation about the role of military tactics in each of their lives. The exchange culminates in the following scene:

> "You know you're really inhuman," the General said.
>
> "Perhaps."
>
> "You never grant a thing, do you?"
>
> Was that what he meant? Hearn stared into his eyes, which were luminous at the moment, almost beseeching. He had an intuition that if he remained motionless long enough the General would slowly extend his arm, touch his knee perhaps.
>
> No that was ridiculous.
>
> But Hearn stood up with a sudden agitated motion, and walked a few steps to the other end of the tent, where he stood motionless for a moment, staring at the General's cot.
>
> His cot. No, get away from there, before Cummings grabbed that interpretation. He wheeled around, and looked at the General who had not moved, had sat like a large and petrified bird, waiting . . . waiting for what must be indefinable. (182)

Hearn's anticipation that the general is not only homosexual but also interested in him emerges quite fully in his thoughts. Hearn's visceral response and his desires remain unclear, though Hearn certainly feels that sex should not occur between them. Provided Hearn harbors homosexual inclinations, his reticence may stem from the prohibition of homosexuality in the armed forces and masculinity in general, the impropriety of the general's close association with a subordinate officer, or Hearn's lack of sexual desire for the general.

The chess scene makes apparent the test of wills prevalent in Cummings and Hearn's relationship, a test that reaches its breaking point in the final scene between the men before Cummings has Hearn transferred out of his service, eventually to Recon, where Hearn perishes on patrol. Immediately preceding this final scene, Hearn snuffs out a cigarette on the floor of the general's tent and leaves both butt and ash for Cummings to discover. Since

Hearn's duty involves the spotless preservation of the general's tent, Hearn realizes the general will know immediately that he left the debris for Cummings to find. When the general does locate Hearn's mess, he experiences a mixed emotional response: "For an instant, deep beneath the currents of his rage, there was another feeling, an odd compound of disgust and fear perhaps, and something else, a curious troubled excitement, a momentary submission as if he had been a young girl undressing before the eyes of a roomful of strange men" (318). Through this reaction Mailer foregrounds the idea that the general's response to Hearn is sexual, beyond the mere commingling of power and desire. The general explores the idea of "submission" to Hearn, sexually, as he imagines becoming a girl naked before him. The fantasy meets with disgust in the general's mind; he dismisses it and determines that in order to preempt its return, he must remove Hearn from his presence.

Mailer's development of the relationship between Cummings and Hearn, though it smacks of homosexuality, never expressly addresses the issue of homosexuality, nor does either character consider himself homosexual. Rather, sexuality is tied to connotations of power. Mailer has asserted that "part of the effectiveness of General Cummings . . . [rests] on the homosexuality I was obviously suggesting as the core of much of his motivation" (*Advertisements* 223). That motivation is so ineluctably connected to the general's psychopathic desire for power that readers can view him as evil because of his lust for power, rather than because of his homosexual inclinations. In this sense the "homosexuality" of the novel belies the novel's realistic classification, refusing to model 1950s conformist culture's condemnation of homosexuality.

In *The Thin Red Line*, by James Jones, the "reality" of homosexuality in the all-male arena of military life is as apparent as other realities, which by the time of its 1962 publication comprised the stock narrative material of war novels. The narrative in Jones's novel occurs on the Pacific island of Guadalcanal, but the battles for the Elephant's Head and the Shrimp's Tail are as contrived as their names. Also like Mailer's soldiers, though less conspicuously and therefore seemingly more genuinely, Jones's Charlie Company personnel microcosmically represent the United States' diversity in geography, race, and religion. Jones draws a dim Kentuckian, Witt; a wide-eyed, marked-for-death Iowan boy, Bead; and a cadre of presumably Italian Brooklynites overly concerned with seeming "hep." The company's original captain, "Bugger" Stein, is a Jew whose compassion for his men prevents him from sending them into conflicts that might result in their deaths. Like Mailer's troupe, Jones's Charlie Company is comprised of seasoned and virginal soldiers, educated and noneducated. Additionally, Jones's characters consciously concern themselves with notions of heroism and bravery, cowardice and fear. For instance, the company's first encounter with combat immobilizes forward clerk Corporal Fife and leaves him aghast at his own response: "Fife would never have believed he could react like this, and he was ashamed of it. It affected the way he regarded everything in life—himself, the sunlight, the blue sky, the trees, skyscrapers, girls. Nothing was beautiful. A desire to be somewhere else constantly trickled up and down his back in vague muscular spasms, even in the daytime. Worse was the knowledge that these violent raging twinges did him no good at all, did not change anything, affected nothing. It was awful to have to admit you were a coward. It meant he would have to work harder at not running away than the others. It was going to be a hard thing to live with, and he knew he had better keep his mouth shut about it and try to hide it" (92).

Though Fife remains mute about his own cowardice, he determines for himself that bravery has no bearing on his actions: "When compared to the fact that he might very well be dead by this time tomorrow, whether he was courageous or not today was pointless, empty" (121). When Fife eventually does relax enough to relay his fear, he learns that he is not alone in his feelings but that to talk about fear "did not help him to tell it. He found that no matter how he overstated it he could not convey the true extent of his fear. It only became funny, when you said it. It wasn't the same thing at all" (148). Fife then discerns a difference between fear in an isolated situation and cowardice as a personal characteristic and discovers he will never be a hero. This does not, however, appear to affect his bearing as a man. In other words, Jones suggests that fear is a realistic element of war that does not ruin heroic moments and is not required for masculine function, ideas certainly anathema to a civilian public who were never allowed to witness soldierly fear. Fife's realization separates him from Brown in *The Naked and the Dead,* who perceives his admission of fear as exoneration for future acts of cowardice.

Jones thus engages with issues of heroism and masculinity much more overtly than Mailer, and the soldiers' preoccupations with their own behaviors comprise a central theme of *The Thin Red Line.* From the outset the characters in Jones's novel recognize the incongruity of war and notions of heroism; they understand that "every old vet is a hero" (23), which implies that acts of heroism are constituted in the retelling. Many of the individual soldiers wonder privately about their own aptitude for battle and ponder repeatedly why they are on Guadalcanal in the first place. Doll asks himself, "What made men do it? . . . What kept them there? Why didn't they just up and leave, all go away?" (37). Doll repeats this question when he learns of Bead's hand-to-hand dispatch of a Japanese soldier: "Doll wondered to himself how men could bring themselves to do such things, and what must it feel like when they did. To find yourself face to face with a screaming Jap bent on killing you and engage with him with naked bayonets" (143). Even after the company members can be called seasoned combatants, Bell questions his motivation to continue and remains unable to locate an impetus specifically: "Whatever it was made him do it . . . he still didn't know" (266).

The one reason that Jones offers for men's willingness to engage in combat is not bravery, but peer pressure. Jones expresses this notion through Fife, who rationalizes his cowardice by examining the consequences he would face if he fails to conquer it. Fife says that "he could think of only one reason why he was here, and that was because he would be ashamed for people to think he was a coward, embarrassed to be put to jail" (122). Later, the same fear of shame motivates Fife's desire to look at the battlefield: "Terrified as he was of standing up and being shot at by some invisible party, he was more terrified of being accused for his cowardice" (145). Even the seasoned veteran Welsh, whose seeming imperviousness to battle (augmented by the canteens he keeps full of gin) resonates among his company mates, understands the social impulsion underlying soldiers' participation in war. Welsh thinks that "all [he] knew was that he was scared shitless, and at the same time was afflicted with a choking gorge of anger that any social coercion existed in the world which could force him to be here" (139). So while the soldiers of Charlie Company recognize their fear and berate themselves for it, Jones's narrative proffers that cowardice is commonplace among soldiers but that man's competitive nature and fear of shame conquer it. In so doing, Jones offers a realistic attempt to explain to civilian America that heroism emerges not from acting bravely but from stifling the human instinct for survival and continuing despite fear. This definition proffers a significant advance upon civilian notions of courage as a quality inherent to soldiers by dint of their service.

Another aspect of war Jones candidly engages involves the connections between war and sex engendered in the energy of battle and in the all-male environs of the military. The men in Jones's novel often characterize battle activities in sexualized terms that would continue to color descriptions of combat significantly in later representations of war. When Charlie Company first approaches battle, the men's faces betray a "breathless, curiously sexual look," which, when they witness another company's engagement, disappears, "replaced by a sullen look of sexual guilt. Nobody seemed to want to meet anybody else's eyes. They looked curiously like a gang of boys caught masturbating together" (69). After killing the Japanese soldier, Bead registers congruent feelings of guilt, which he elucidates in sexual terms: "Maybe my mother beat me up too many times for jerking off when I was a kid!" (179). Additionally, when trying to rationalize his elation during points of high battle stress, Private Bell can only compare the feeling to one he experienced as a youth while masturbating in an outdoor location where he risked discovery. Once able to connect the two scenes, Bell accounts for his combat emotions in sexual terms: "His climb out into the trough that first time, even his participation in the failed assault, all were—in some way he could not fully understand—sexual, and as sexual, and in much the same way, as his childhood incident of the gravelled road" (285). The stimulation Bell receives from combat rivals that he receives from sex.

Though each of these comparisons focuses upon the fear of being caught masturbating, the pervasiveness of sexual feeling generated by war also brings to the fore the desire for intercourse, simmering in the war setting. Whereas Mailer's work acknowledges his characters as sexual beings in their "Time Machine" segments, their sexual feelings appear to have vanished or been deeply repressed in battle, as evidenced on the one hand by the Recon soldiers' total lack of expression and on the other by the general's outright denial of such feelings in his treatment of Hearn. Mailer's soldiers emerge as chaste as those soldiers the Office of War Information allowed civilians to view. Moreover, *The Naked and the Dead* rarely features relative levels of undress, a censorship as total as that the Office of War Information exercised over "sexually ambivalent images" (Roeder 49). Jones, on the other hand, frequently describes the soldiers working with few or no clothes at all, as when Charlie Company first lands on Guadalcanal and takes in the scene before them: "[The soldiers] were in all stages of dress and undress, sleeveless shirts, legless pants, no shirts at all, and in some few cases, particularly those working in or near the water, they worked totally stark naked or in their white government issue underpants through which the dark hairiness of their genitals showed plainly" (38). Moreover, Jones does not recoil from descriptions with sexual undertones. When describing conditions in the ship's hold before Charlie Company lands on the island, Jones notes "the olfactory numbness caused by the saturation of breath, feet, armpits and crotches" (2). Mailer's description of the same location centers on "stale cooking—fat mixed with something as nauseous as the curds from a grease trap" (307). While Jones allows the men to have bodies and to view one another in suggestively homoerotic modes, Mailer prohibits these implications in his text. The reality Jones portrays includes male-male affection, the presence of sexual desire, and even homosexual activity in the military setting, and thus actively resists civilian imagistic indoctrination.

Jones describes male-male affection in *The Thin Red Line* in the form of the male bond in a war setting. Soldiers develop affectionate feelings toward the members of their immediate platoon or company, which they often describe as having greater intensity than those they feel for their lovers. Lieutenant Band expresses such sentiments: "There was . . . a mysterious quality of deepest, most manly friendship which could exist between men who shared the pain and death, the fear and the sadness of combat—and the happiness, too. For there was happiness. Happiness in doing your best, happiness in fighting by the side of your friend. Band did not know where this powerful, manly friendship came from, or what exactly caused it, but he knew that it existed and there were times when Band felt closer to the men in his outfit than he had ever felt to his wife" (101).

Private Witt also admits to these intense male-bonding relationships, albeit in a less introspective manner: "The truth was, [he] loved them all, passionately, with an almost sexual ecstasy of comradeship" (319). Upon returning to Charlie Company after one of his quasi-desertions, Witt feels that he "could have thrown his arms around his commander and kissed him on his dirt-crusted stubbled cheek in an ecstasy of loving comradeship" (324). Witt refrains, however, because "it might have looked faggoty, or get taken the wrong way" (324). Witt's reluctance establishes the crucial difference between comradely relations of an intense nature and homosexual attraction, a distinction that sometimes gets elided in the soldiers' interactions with one another. The problem with narrating such episodes (for both Witt as a character and Jones as author) is that in a postwar civilian setting "male-

male affection," especially once it reaches a level of physical intimacy, can only translate into "homosexuality" for both the activity and the participants. Though not entirely introspective, Witt senses this predicament and judges in favor of the prohibition.

This is not to claim, however, that homosexuality does not exist in *The Thin Red Line*. Men known to be homosexuals form the novel's Cannon Company: "the worst drunkards, worst homosexuals, and worst troublemakers all gathered together under one roof" (105). Witt's association with Cannon Company influences his fear of being *perceived* as a homosexual. Jones's use of the superlative "worst" indicates that some homosexuals were not transferred to Cannon Company, suggesting a hierarchy of sexual identities that itself confirms their presence.

The men who engage in homosexual activity in Jones's text seem acutely aware of how their actions may be perceived both by outsiders and by the rest of the military establishment. Two such men are tent mates Fife and Bead, who share a series of sexual encounters. Bead instigates their initial encounter after "he had come crawling in at a moment when Fife, already disrobed to his underwear, had been thinking ardently about girls" (125). Bead pretends not to notice Fife's erection, but once the two bed down, Bead suggests that since there are no girls present, the boys ought to take care of one another. Fife consents, and the boys fellate one another. In all, the boys have sex with one another four times.

Several dynamics between the soldiers seem geared to rationalize the relationship for the characters themselves and in the text as a whole. First, Jones characterizes Bead as a boy, and though older, Fife also retains a boyish quality, especially in the distinction he draws between himself and the men he perceives as heroic. Jones thus implies that sex between boys—that is, "kid stuff"—registers as less offensive than that between men. Second, the boys justify assisting one another in getting off through the absence of female companionship. When Fife considers their experiences, his thoughts indicate not only that he's familiar with homosexual relations in the military but that he knows how and why they develop. Fife uses his knowledge to exonerate himself from the guilt attendant upon homosexual activity:

All he knew was that he did not feel guilty about what he did with Bead. He felt he ought to feel guilty. But the truth was that he didn't. After all, what was the difference between doing the same things now that you did as a kid, and doing them when you were a freshman or sophomore. Only all the talk you had heard in the meantime about fairies and queers. Fife knew there were oldtimers in the army who had their young boyfriends whom they slept with as with a wife. In return, the young soldiers received certain favors from their protectors, not the least of which was more money to spend on women in town. None of this buggering was considered homosexual by anyone and authority turned a blind eye to it. But that was buggering. On the other hand there were the overt homosexuals, much increased since the drafting of civilians, whom everybody disliked, though many might avail themselves of their services. (127–28)

His awareness of homosexual relations in the military allows Fife to accept what has transpired between himself and Bead, as if the circumstances themselves justify the act, and so long as he knows they're not the only soldiers who engage in such activity. Peter Jones writes that "it is plain in context that pragmatic expediency and urgent pressures from the proverbial 'rusty load' are their motivation, that under normal circumstances neither would resort to homosexual practices" (117). Nevertheless, James Jones presents sex between men as a military fact known to all soldiers as blatantly as he presents stock narrative characteristics. This presentation excuses homosexual activities when they're a result of military circumstance, a last resort. But the fact that James Jones exonerates those soldiers involved in homosexual activity and assuages concern over how they'll behave in "normal" circumstances encourages civilians to overlook their behavior as well. James Jones thus accomplishes a reevaluation of the soldiers' activities that at least allows room for their continued masculine function.

Whereas Fife countenances his sexual relationship with Bead, denying its implications, Private Doll halts his pursuit of Carol "Carrie" Arbre when he discerns the effects their union would have on his identity. Arguably the most intriguing factor in the developing relationship between Doll and Carrie is Jones's characterization of Arbre's "girlish" body (414)—a body that automatically makes the men of the company think he's homosexual. Jones introduces Arbre as "a rather girlishly-built, girlish-looking young man, who was continually having his bottom felt in joke or perhaps not in joke[.] Arbre had been forced throughout his Army career to protest furiously against such indignities. People could not believe, given his girlish build, that he was not homosexually inclined" (414). When the two men defilade themselves from mortar shelling, Doll accidentally lands atop Carrie and, pressing his crotch to Arbre's buttocks, realizes that they are "rather sweet" (415). To his surprise, Doll also realizes that even though the mortar shelling stops, the pleasure he felt when pressed to Carrie lingers. Doll thus sets out upon a pursuit of Carrie's butt: "Sweating blood, or feeling as if he were, he lay and stared at it until it became his own, his possession. And he knew from some heretofore unreached depth within himself that he wanted to make love to it—physical, gentle, fondling, sexual love" (477).

Peter Jones characterizes Doll's pursuit of Arbre as "pure comedy" (117), but the affectional characterization of Doll's courtship problematizes the reader's ability to see only comedy or a situational dynamic.[8] Doll is not interested in simply getting off; he wants to consummate an affair with Arbre. His desire remains long after the shelling has stopped and is, therefore, not definable in terms of the sexual energy elicited through battle. Doll does attempt to render his desire acceptable. Since he outranks Carrie, Doll considers "pogeying" Arbre, that is, offering him favors such as protection in return for an ongoing sexual exchange. Doll considers this hierarchy because it "didn't make *him* homosexual. It only made Arbre homosexual, if he accepted it—and Doll was certain Arbre would accept it" (477, emphasis in original). When Doll finally attempts to seduce Arbre, his sense that Arbre would consent is proven true, but the roles he has imagined for each of them are not: when Carrie whips open his trousers and invites Doll to service him, Doll realizes that Arbre has long considered Doll homosexual as well. In order to stem that assumption, Doll must suppress his desire, which effectively ends his obsession with Carrie. For Doll the consummation can only happen if he doesn't emerge as homosexual.

The implication that mutual consent to the relationship would constitute *both* men as homosexual in civilian terms informs Doll's curtailed pursuit—though Doll clearly desires Arbre, he desires being seen as homosexual less. His reluctance stems from public, civilian censure; military exigencies can accommodate the behavior within prescribed boundaries. Because James Jones presents homosexual seduction and activity in *The Thin Red Line,* the novel declares these aspects of military life—aspects for which civilian consciousness could not yet account—real. Moreover, Jones's characters, like Hemingway's in *The Sun Also Rises,* understand how behaviors between men signify differently in military and civilian contexts.[9] While the sexual encounters between Bead and Fife can be dismissed as "boy stuff," and therefore signify less in terms of masculinity, the relational development between Doll and Arbre can be read as one in which Doll falls in love with another man. That this trajectory of desire must be thwarted indicates Jones's awareness of the threat homosexuality posed to ideas about masculinity in postwar conformist culture, but his realistic portrayal of wartime encourages civilian Americans to view homosexual activity and desire as part of the function of soldiers and thus aligned with the soldier-hero designation civilian culture grants. By positing that homosexual activities and desires occur for the soldier-hero without detracting from his masculine function, Jones encourages a broadened definition of manhood in terms the civilian culture will likely find sympathetic.

## The Gay Novel: *Playboy,* Bachelor Culture, and Envisioning a Masculine Gay Male

Whereas renegade forms of masculinity celebrated in motorcycle gangs, juvenile delinquency, and James Dean rebel imagery harkened back to the homosocial environs offered by military life that Mailer and Jones revisit, explorations of alternate forms of masculinity also emerged in the 1950s rise of bachelor culture. Bachelor culture offered men an avenue for assimilation into consumer culture without the concomitant demand for suburban domesticity. The principle image associated with bachelor culture in the 1950s was *Playboy* magazine. Beth Bailey recounts how *Playboy* was "begun by Hugh Hefner in 1953 with an initial print run of 70,000" and notes that it "passed the one million circulation mark in three years" (247). *Playboy* "represented bachelorhood as a form of male liberation from domestic ideology from the outset" (Cohan 30) by combining an unqualified support of masculine independence with an overt disavowal of the single man's homosexuality: pictures of nude women. And the ideal of bachelorhood took hold. In *The Hearts of Men* Barbara Ehrenreich claims that *Playboy* "proposed an alternative way of life that became ever more concrete and vivid as the years went on" (49).

This "alternative way of life" nevertheless participated in postwar consumerist culture because along with it came the requisite accoutrements frequently advertised in magazines. For example, in 1956 *Playboy* ran a spread entitled "Penthouse Apartment for a Bachelor" that depicted an array of domestic products along with the keys to a Jaguar, held on a *Playboy* key ring (Sanders 54), suggesting the heterosexuality of the 1950s bachelor. Such imagistic coding was necessary to prevent the public perception that choices of predominantly male companionship, decorative self-styling, and domestic consumer spending—in short, the effeminization of men—also signaled a man's homosexuality.

Early gay novelists appear to work within the paradigm of the signifying systems inaugurated by *Playboy* and bachelor culture, but they do so with the ostensible aim of interrupting how ideals of masculinity and femininity operated in the culture at large. If, as *Playboy* asserted, men could still be men while adopting some hitherto feminine characteristics, perhaps, the novelists imagined, the time was ripe to dismantle the hetero-/homo- binary preventing gay men from signifying as masculine. To this end, novels like Gore Vidal's *The City and the Pillar* and James Barr's *Quatrefoil* challenged conformist culture ideas about gender by positing an alternative soldierly masculinity for gay soldiers. Like the realist novels of Mailer and Jones, *The City and the Pillar* and *Quatrefoil* revert to World War II's all-male environment to explore male homosexuality and to ask readers to consider the gay protagonists masculine simply because they are soldiers who disavow traditionally feminine mannerisms and behaviors.

The protagonists of Gore Vidal's *The City and the Pillar* and James Barr's *Quatrefoil* accept their homosexual identities and the social stigma attendant upon them. Vidal and Barr thus present these men as sympathetic characters, and the novels seem intent on quelling negative public perceptions of homosexuality by casting it within the realm of soldierly service, a setting that automatically confers manhood in the civilian mindset. The emancipatory space for homosexuals the novels imagine specifically connects homosexuality to soldierly masculinity, and in turn to national allegiance, perhaps to dissolve the links between homosexuals and communists foregrounded during the 1950s hearings of the House Un-American Activities Committee (HUAC). The gay protagonists of *The City and the Pillar* and *Quatrefoil* seem intentionally characterized to conquer what Robert Corber identifies as "the only way in which homosexuality could become a topic of debate in the political public sphere," which was "as a form of psychopathology that threatened national security" (85).

Unfortunately, as this section will demonstrate, like the unrealized consummation of a relationship between Doll and Carrie in *The Thin Red Line,* these novels violently thwart "successful" homosexual identity and effectively reify both traditional modes of masculine signification and the psychopathological discourse of homosexuality Corber describes in Cold War America. These narrative developments suggest that Vidal and Barr discerned that the time of liberation, of resignifying masculinity, had not yet arrived—indeed, could not be imagined in the conformist social milieu of the 1950s, which desired only domesticated men.

Gore Vidal's 1948 publication of *The City and the Pillar* protests the contemporaneous psychopathological model for comprehending homosexuality and hence uses the war narrative to correct what Vidal sees as a civilian misunderstanding of the soldier. As Robert Corber suggests, "Vidal . . . originally wrote the novel to undermine the set of narratives available for representing gay male experience, narratives that reduced gay male identity to a form of gender inversion" (136). Vidal challenges such narratives through Jim Willard, an athletic and, for all intents and purposes, "normal" middle-class boy. *The City and the Pillar* thus protests 1950s conformist culture by positing the military's place for male-male relations as the site for creating a civilian homosexual identity for Jim that allows his continued definition as a man.

Jim's enlistment in the military symbolically bisects the novel's narrative trajectory into Jim's life prior to his acquiescence to his homosexual identity and his life afterward. Vidal makes the transition clear when he writes that in "December when the United States went to war with Japan . . . they were once more part of the world" (105). Prior to December 1941, Jim, along with writer Paul Sullivan and socialite Maria Verlaine, reside in the Yucatan. Though Paul and Jim are lovers at this time, Paul has intentionally introduced Jim to Verlaine because of his residual belief that she might "rescue" him from the homosexual underworld existent outside their idyllic Mexican haven. Paul believes that due to his masculine bearing, Jim could never truly love a man, so he holds out the hope that Jim will locate the right woman. Believing that woman to be Maria Verlaine, Paul pushes Jim toward her. He says: "I thought it would be the best thing that could happen to you. She's a wonderful woman. She can get you out of this world." To which Jim responds, "Why should I get out?" (107). This question comprises his acknowledgment of his homosexual identity. When almost immediately thereafter Jim concedes to a feeling of having been "released" from their trio "by the fact of war," he claims he "would soon be resolved by action. He could not wait for his own life to begin" (109). Thus, Jim equates his future military service with the beginning of his life and in so doing reflects the civilian mindset linking manhood with participation in war.

But Jim does all of this without the thought that he'll "get out" of a homosexual identity. Unlike Paul, Jim believes he is capable of loving another man, for he has already chosen that man in the character of Bob Ford. Growing up together, Jim and Bob had a sexual rendezvous shortly before Bob departed to join the Merchant Marine. For Jim this experience portends not so much his developing identity as his quest throughout the narrative to establish a permanent basis for their relationship, both physically and emotionally. The quest invokes Plato's conception of lovers introduced in the *Symposium*, for Jim recalls that when he lay with Bob on the banks of the stream, "they were complete, each became the other, as their bodies collided with a primal violence, like to like, metal to magnet, half to half and the whole restored" (25). Jim's quest to restore that feeling of wholeness with Bob carries him throughout the narrative.

Since Bob is a year ahead of Jim in school, Jim must remain behind to earn his diploma while Bob enlists in the Merchant Marine. When Jim does not hear from Bob in his year's absence, Jim becomes a sailor in hopes of eventually catching up with Bob. Jim abandons his sailing life when one of his fellow seamen calls him a "queer" for not wishing to have sex with girls the two meet in port. At this point Jim's homosexual identity is not fully formed, or is at least not one he is prepared to accept: "At the moment when what should have happened was about to happen, the image of Bob had come between him and the girl, rendering the act obscene and impossible. . . . Yet he realized that it would be a difficult matter to live in a world of men and women without participating in their ancient and necessary duet. Was he able to participate? Yes, he decided, under other circumstances. In any case, the word Collins had shouted after him was hardly apt" (48).

Scared of the implications of Collins's epithet and unwilling, as yet, to accept whatever truth it might contain, Jim moves to Hollywood and begins work as a tennis instructor at the Garden Hotel in Beverly Hills, where he encounters the homosexual underworld. The homosexual bellhops at the hotel invite Jim to attend parties with them, and "finally, one tried to seduce him" (56). Like any man as yet unwilling to accept his own homosexuality, Jim "was quite unnerved, and violent in his refusal" (56). While Jim's refusal ostensibly relates to the "disgust and alarm" he feels after his "discovery that there were indeed many men who liked other men" (56), in reality Jim despises the mannerisms that identify the men as homosexual more than the sexual activity itself. He notes that "his new companions puzzled him. Their conversation was often cryptic, their eyes quick-moving, searching. Ill at ease with outsiders, they were quarrelsome with one another" (55). And Jim "made no connection between what he and Bob had done and what his new acquaintances did. Too many of them behaved like women" (62).

However, when his companions introduce him to handsome actor Ronald Shaw at one of the underworld's parties, Jim determines he has met a different sort of homosexual, for, like Jim, Shaw "hate[s] those others, those lousy queens." In imitation "Shaw [lifts] one shoulder and [gives] a curiously feminine shake to his body, mocking in a single gesture the entire legion" (65). Jim and Shaw esteem their own homosexual feelings over those of other men because of the mere fact of their masculine bearing. Shaw sums up the distinction when he claims that "if a man likes men, he wants a man, and if he likes women, he wants a woman, so who wants a freak who's neither?" (66). Robert Corber reads the distinctions drawn here by Shaw and Jim as indicative of Vidal's attempt to separate sexuality from gender identity, thus offering an alternative to the pathological model of the homosexual as a female trapped within a male body. But Vidal's text still rather homophobically assents to *some* people's homoerotic desires, while degrading those of others, though such privileging is in keeping with hierarchies of gendered identities still extant today. I would like instead to suggest, then, that Jim and Shaw's disgust with the queens represents Vidal's attempt to repudiate Cold War discontinuities between masculinity and homosexuality. Vidal believes that society might be able to accept homosexuals provided they behave like men, just as Jones imagined veterans could retain masculinity, even heroism, though they might experience fear or homosexual activity. These fantasies of acceptance emerge directly out of the war experience, and the novels, as I read them, attempt to use the civilian link between masculinity and soldiering to expand definitions of successful manhood. In particular, the novels imagine that if soldiers could engage in homosexual activity and still function as soldiers, as men, then they might also appear manly to civilians—hence Vidal's attempt to distinguish homosexuals by their gendered behaviors: the masculine gay man stood a better chance of civilian masculine definition.

It is no wonder, then, that Vidal follows Jim's connection to "manly" homosexuals such as Shaw and Sullivan with his entrance into the military.

Like many American men Jim enlists because he "had some strange idea that [he'd] be useful" (112). As in Mailer's and Jones's novels, Jim's military experience includes encounters with homosexuals. Jim is "very much aware of those alert-looking soldiers, forever searching for a response" (115). He develops a crush on one of the pilots, "a roaring boy with blond hair who was particularly popular with the ground crews. He sang popular songs in a loud toneless voice, indulged in horse-play and generally gave pleasure. Once Jim found himself face to face with him. Jim saluted, but the pilot only grinned and clapped him on the shoulder and said 'Hi!' One boy to another. Jim was dazzled. And that was all. Rank separated them. It was sad" (115).

But not all of Jim's encounters remain surreptitious, nor do his desires remain unrequited. His immediate supervisor, Sergeant Kervinski, attempts to seduce him one night over dinner. Vidal describes how "he winked and Jim was disgusted," Jim reflecting that "although it was impossible for anyone in the Army to be honest about such things, at least there were more straight-forward ways of going about a seduction" (118). Uninterested in Kervinski, Jim instead watches a handsome corporal he sees across the room: "He was a dark-haired boy with gray eyes and a small slim body that looked strong. Watching him through half-closed eyes, Jim felt desire. For the first time in months he wanted sex. He wanted the young corporal. Mentally, he raped him, made love to him, worshipped him; they would be brothers and never parted" (120). Jim later fails in an attempt to seduce the corporal, Ken, and discovers that Sergeant Kervinski once succeeded in doing so.

As the final attraction Jim feels for another man while in the service, Jim's desire for Ken is instructive for a number of reasons. First, in light of Kervinski's success, Jim's thwarted seduction of Ken indicates Jim's status as a novice in the art of homosexual seduction, the very thing for which Jim criticizes Kervinski—for while Kervinski is clearly a less attractive and more effete man than Jim, he has seduced Ken. Second, Jim imagines Ken in the place he has always reserved for Bob, as his brother and permanent partner. Finally, Jim's fantasizing reflects the violence associated with homosexuality throughout the text and foreshadows his eventual reunion with Bob.

In the initial published version of *The City and the Pillar* (1948), when the boyhood lovers again meet, Jim rapes and murders Bob when the latter does not wish to resume their sexual relationship. Vidal eventually revised and rereleased *The City and the Pillar* (1965), retaining the rape but editing out the murder. While the later edition may reduce what Claude Summers calls the "melodramatic" (75) character of the novel's original ending, it re-iterates the original version's classification of homosexuality as pathological. Granted, Vidal forwards the image of a masculine homosexual. Unfortunately, however, the persistent relationship between violence and homosexuality still renders Jim pathological, only in different terms. Jim and Bob initially connect with "primal violence" (25); when Jim is propositioned by one of the bellhops at the Garden Hotel, he is "violent in his refusal" (56); when he imagines sex with Ken, he fantasizes raping him (120); and finally, Jim rapes Bob when the latter calls him "queer" (191) for grabbing hold of his penis while they lie together after their reunion. This violent pathologizing of homosexuality renders the preliberatory attitude Corber finds in this text mute. The homosexual Jim Willard locates no place for his identity in the postwar culture. Therefore, the novel posits that homosexuality, regardless of its attempted connection to masculinity, remains too threatening to allow. As Summers asserts, "The novel defines freedom as not having to tell lies, but it also soberly recognizes that, for the gay man or lesbian in 1948 America, freedom is far from reality" (59). While it appears as if Jim only desires a lasting relationship with a soul-mate, his means of obtaining that relationship and his reactions to his homosexuality situate him fully within the dominant narrative of homosexual pathology.

The freedom of a contented homosexual relationship also remains too unrealistic and too threatening for James Barr to imagine in his 1950 novel *Quatrefoil*. Certainly the least well-known of these novels, Barr's text begins at the end of World War II, the point when civilian America began accommodating the return of veterans and the resultant shifts in expectations of men. *Quatrefoil* focuses on an inappropriate relationship between an officer and an enlisted man. Navy ensign Phillip Froelich returns from war in 1946 to face court-martial proceedings for insubordination. While on board Phillip had challenged and disobeyed his superior officer in an attempt to protect Stuff Manus, the sailor with whom he had nearly had homosexual contact. The two had initially befriended each other ostensibly because Phillip wanted to help the illiterate Manus learn to read. However, during a storm when the two worked the deck together, Stuff's bare chest brushed against Froelich's bare back in a manner reminiscent of Doll and Carrie Arbre's circumstantial contact. When Froelich met Manus's eyes, he discovered the intention of the touch. According to military protocol and his own notions of morality, Phillip deflected Manus's advances and curtailed their friendship. Barr writes that "because of that moment their friendship, forbidden by naval regulation between officers and the men they commanded, no longer existed" (5). When recalling the incident to Commander Tim Danelaw later in the novel, Phillip admits that he was "shocked and amused" but that he "should have discussed it, pointing out that the unnatural, all-male society in which we lived had germinated such emotions" (136). The statement expresses Froelich's belief that, though apparent in the military, such relationships would desist afterward—the men's respective ranks, not their genders, prohibit their relationship. Barr, like Jones, attempts to assuage civilian doubts about the persistence of male-male affection or homosexuality in postwar America, doubts compounded into threats by the HUAC hearings, which sought to expose homosexuals because their putative susceptibility to blackmail was believed to constitute a threat to national security. Barr dramatizes these historical events, likely familiar to his readers, when Manus blackmails Phillip, but he also encourages readers' sympathy for the human emotions involved. Readers witness the emotional difficulty of Phillip's pending court-martial, while they also come to understand how nonthreatening homosexual activity really was to national security.

Because of the implications of homosexuality directed at Phillip, Tim Danelaw, Phillip's commanding officer and a closeted homosexual himself, sees to it that the court-martial proceedings against Phillip are terminated, and the rest of the novel involves Phillip and Tim's developing relationship. The homosexual relations between the men are not consummated until far into the novel, as Phillip clings to the notion that "one became degenerate or one didn't, as he chose" (73). Prior to consummation their relationship registers to others as mere male-male affection, a sort of closely bonded mentoring of a junior man by his senior. Meanwhile, Tim introduces Phillip to the homosexual underworld and its hidden codes and signals.

Because of the mentor/student dynamic and the fact that Tim is married and Phillip engaged, Barr depicts homosexuality not as an identity but as the men's full intellectual development. As such, Tim serves as Phillip's moral, intellectual, and creative guide throughout the course of the novel, and their friendship figures much like ancient Greek models of homosexuality. By anesthetizing homosexual relations as men's access to higher modes of being, instead of pathologizing them as sexual licentiousness, Barr presents a desire to make homosexuality acceptable to postwar conformist culture. This parlay is made especially clear through the men's membership in the armed forces. The navy, after all, first introduced Phillip to Stuff Manus and to the possibility of a male-male affectional relationship developing a homosexual character, and the navy fosters Phillip's exploration of such relationships with Tim Danelaw. However, throughout nearly the entire novel Phillip insists that such relationships remain within the cynosure of the military. Once returned to civilian life, Phillip intends to marry and live a life above reproach, in other words, a life of conformity.

To emphasize the compulsion to conformity, Barr characterizes Phillip through modes of traditional contemporaneous thought. Phillip loathes infidelity in Pat, Commander Danelaw's wife, with whom he has an affair, but fails to place the same onus of judgment upon himself. He expresses discomfort at modern ballet and architecture and at women's use of profanity. As such, Phillip emerges as antimodern. Tim, on the other hand, reeks of modernity. He boasts a large emerald pinky ring, enjoys art, and resides in a fantastically modern house. These distinctions between traditional and modern also frequently align themselves with those between masculine and feminine. Tim, as an artist, is considered fey, and "like most men of his class, [Phillip] considered art effeminate" (122). Phillip appreciates his own predilections over those of Danelaw, because *effeminate* is "the most damning adjective in his vocabulary" (122). Moreover, Phillip recognizes an immanent need to retain the masculine bearing upon which he prides himself, for he believes, like Vidal's Jim Willard, that what must be preserved above all else is society's perception of him as manly, as masculine.

But Phillip feels more than just an intellectual draw to Tim, and vice versa. Phillip considers how he might use Tim's attraction: "Many years ago, and without too many serious qualms, Phillip had admitted to himself that certain men found him more than interesting. He looked upon this fact as a potential weapon which he might better use to his own advantage rather than have it used against him" (54). Phillip precludes the possibility of a mutual interest that both parties clearly wish to pursue, largely because like most in Cold War America, Phillip believes homosexuality to be both chosen and pathological. He expresses these attitudes throughout the text. As already noted, he feels that the choice to be homosexual is the choice to "become degenerate." Phillip classifies his homoerotic desires as "an ugliness inside him, a scar tissue on his brain" (24), and claims that Tim "was a reminder of an undisciplined element in his personality that Phillip wanted to conceal" (31). In what might be considered either pathological self-loathing or homosexual panic (generally motivated by homosexuality itself), Phillip imagines the homosexual as "indecent, ugly, and diseased, and perverted" (169).

Phillip eventually owns up to his attraction for Tim and the homosexual nature of it. Like the brother-twin presentation Vidal fashions of Jim and Bob, Tim and Phillip are characterized as "so much alike . . . that at times [Phillip] felt they had practiced the narrower rites of Narcissus rather than those of homosexuality. It was as if in exploring each other, each of them discovered something of himself he had not yet learned to love" (197). Further, Barr's design, like Vidal's, foregrounds both men's masculine characteristics—they are brothers. Neither one suffers from gender inversion, even if Tim's a bit flamboyant. The realization of his possible homosexuality is not an easy one for Phillip, however, as he feels himself to be "mentally ill" and harboring a "dangerous, but usual combination" (313) of homosexuality and melancholia. The account of Phillip's coming to terms with his own homosexuality reads more like a philosophical treatise on how a homosexual justifies his existence than like the depiction of an entrée into a liberated life of self-acceptance. The terms of this treatise emerge in a discussion Tim and Phillip undertake while the latter attempts to discern his future course. Phillip says: "Suppose I granted you . . . that homosexuality is justifiable in certain instances and under certain controls. Then here is the catch: where does justification end and degeneracy begin? Society must condemn to protect. Permit even the intellectual homosexual a place of respect and the first bar is down. Then come the next and the next until the sadist, the flagellist, the criminally insane demand their places, and society ceases to exist" (310). This slippery-slope logic once again introduces Cold War America's belief in the threat homosexuality offered to conformist culture, and it models many debates over changes in social acceptance of the previously marginalized. The degenerate was classified specifically as a gender invert, so masculinity too emerges as threatened by homosexuality. Though Tim wishes for Phillip to attain his highest level of conscious development, Phillip remains unpersuaded.

Ironically, the deciding factor in Phillip and Tim's eventual commingling of lives comes from Phillip's sister Fanchon. Whereas 1950s conformist culture relied upon the nuclear family as a protective barrier against homosexuality, Phillip's family instead entices him into pursuing a relationship with Danelaw and promises that whenever he wants to return to the family's home in Oklahoma, his inheritance will be secure. Fanchon's support suggests Barr's idea of the proper familiar response to a homosexual member's coming out. With his sister's sanction Phillip returns to Tim, and the liberated union comes when the men escape to Tim's Canadian island retreat. Phillip tells Tim, and through Barr conformist culture as a whole, how he has come to accept his own homosexuality: "Homosexuality or anything else is justifiable when it frees the intellect which can only go so far and then finds itself stopped. Then the vice becomes a vehicle of release. The sin lies not in the vice, but in the individual's failure to encompass it and live with it" (343). The pursuit of excellence in mind and body that this theory outlines also resonates with appropriately masculine endeavors, with the expectation of personal excellence frequently attached to military service members. Phillip's resolution seems guaranteed, the setting idyllic, the future promising.

Two days later Tim dies in a plane wreck. The death once again establishes the sinister connection between a liberated homosexual identity and brutal violence proffered in *The City and the Pillar* and suggests that 1950s culture allowed no narrative space for such images of liberation because of their threat both to Cold War culture and to civilian definitions of masculinity. Though Phillip once claimed that a life with Tim offered him but two destinies, mediocrity or disaster, and that he could not "accept one without a knowledge of the other" (184), the narrative trajectory affirms that disaster in fact constitutes his only possible destiny. Readers must wonder, as Phillip does, whether choosing safety over happiness might have prevented Tim's appalling demise. In its narrative resolution the novel acknowledges Cold War culture's demand for conformity, a life of mediocrity that refused to challenge traditions and barriers.[10] For those who transgressed, violent disaster was imminent. *Quatrefoil* protests the strictures of conformist culture by presenting sympathetic characters who struggle with self-definition yet experience emotional pain and suffering for choosing to pursue love relationships that society condemns.

Like the works of Mailer and Jones, Vidal's and Barr's novels reflect the apprehension of a culture at war with itself over definitions of masculinity. Ill content to let the soldier-hero be torn asunder by the domesticated conformist man, the novelists all invite Cold War culture to expand its definition of masculinity by reverting to war, the arena where American culture had long conferred a man's status. Thus, by attempting to reimagine World War II for civilian audiences, the novelists hope to lay claim to presentations of the war previously unknown on the home front and thus, by bridging the gap between civilian and soldierly experience, to recuperate and expand the figure of the soldier-hero as society's definition of a man. They could not foresee, however, that America's next major conflict, the Vietnam War, would quickly dismantle any notion of a heroic masculinity for the civilian public, who would vilify and blame the soldier for a failed war. Finding heroism devoid of signification, soldiers would retreat to simple self-preservation as the way to execute the war, and the conflict itself would signify not in terms of the soldier-hero's victory, but in terms of whether or not he survived and how.

# THE BRIDGE
# TO VIETNAM

*The War Story and
AWOL Masculinity*

Because of its relatively late appearance (1961), nonlinear narrative style, and dubious representation of historical fact and chronology, critics have been hard-pressed to refer to Joseph Heller's *Catch-22* as a World War II novel, and the book's repeated references to exigencies of Cold War America do not help clarify matters. David Seed indicates that "the constant references to conspiracy relate the novel to postwar America" and points out that "Heller inserts references to IBM machines, helicopters and the political developments in America of the 1950s" (68). Because of these details Seed claims that "the reader can neither naturalise the setting nor the period of its action since it incorporates material from two very different eras" (58). But naturalizing setting and action clearly is not Heller's intent. Heller himself once claimed, in an interview for *Playboy* magazine, that "*Catch-22* wasn't really *about* World War II. It was really about American society during the Cold War, during the Korean War, and about the possibility of a Vietnam" (Sam Merrill 68, emphasis in original). Indeed, the novel aims to make what readers know about World War II foreign by making conditions of Cold War life in the United States too familiar—conditions such as paranoia over imminent death, created by the ever-escalating arms race between the United States and the Soviet Union. So the novel both responds to the postwar civilian need to understand World War II anew and offers its own revisionist view of the war. This revisionist view reflects Cold War modes of understanding: that war is without notions of heroic or masculine honor; that truth is constructed, often fabricated out of air; that the individual lacks meaning in a bureaucratically regimented society and in the scope of larger economic and political projects; and that military hierarchies designed to protect U.S. interests and forward American ideals are instead staffed by pompous, ignorant careerists. These ideas would certainly gain credence later in the decade of the novel's publication as a way of thinking about the war in Vietnam.

In the process of exposing these ideas about war, Joseph Heller simultaneously works within a tradition of war writing and transforms that tradition to such an extent that elements of *Catch-22* would become tropes for later representations of war. This chapter labels Heller's novel a "bridge" to Vietnam for three interrelated reasons. First, it serves as a historical bridge—the access to contemporaneous cultural awareness that the novel provides amalgamates its World War II setting, Korean War events, and Cold War attitudes, while also presaging settings, events, and attitudes of the Vietnam War. Second, the novel acts as an imagistic bridge that links questions of soldierly masculinity arising in the World War II novels discussed in the previous chapter with John Yossarian's dereliction of duty. Yossarian's escape at novel's end imagines an AWOL masculinity, a nonheroic hero who would become a trope of war representations for the remainder of the twentieth century and into the twenty-first. And finally, as the chapter's title implies, the novel functions as an ideological bridge, fulfilling the imperative created by other texts discussed in *Male Armor*—Heller's novel bridges the gap between civilian understanding and soldierly experience of war by literally juxtaposing civilian and soldier casualties in the expectation that the reader's repugnance at the death of civilian "innocents" will carry over to his/her attitudes toward the soldiers who die one by one, seemingly without reason and in service of no noble cause.

*Catch-22* initially seems nearly incomprehensible because of Heller's style, which is characterized by repetitive phrasing, rapid-fire slapstick dialogue, fragmented narrative, and cinematic jumps in time and space. But when extracted from its nonlinear presentation, the plot follows the military career of a B-25 bombardier named John Yossarian, from his basic training in Colorado, through his flight school in Santa Ana, California, to his deployment at the European front on the island of Pianosa. As Michael Scoggins relates, "Pianosa is a real island, situated between the large islands of Corsica and Elba in the Ligurian Sea off the northwest coast of Italy" (214). Yossarian's Pianosa resembles Heller's own station on Corsica, from which Heller flew sixty missions for the U.S. Army Air Corps (Scoggins 214). A series of mid-air misadventures, coupled with the escalating mortality rates of his compeers, convinces Yossarian to find a means to avoid missions or to transfer home. *Catch-22* dramatizes the various attempts Yossarian makes to shirk his duty, including faking illness, altering maps of unconquered territory, walking backward or naked through the base camp, and refusing to fly.

Ostensibly, the setting is World War II: "The number of missions required of the aircrews in *Catch-22* is an accurate reflection of the reality of the war in southern Europe" (Scoggins 216). But the war as described in the novel is curiously devoid of specific historical references, especially any reference to the ideals for which the war was fought—to combat the spread of Fascism and Nazism and to end Hitler's brutalizing and inhumane concentration camps. Heller thus accomplishes a rescripting of World War II that denies civilian connection to the nobility of cause, and this rescripting links his novel to the ideological aspirations of other World War II novels discussed in the previous chapter.

Moreover, the time frame of the novel is complicated through references to advancements in Cold War–era technology, such as computers and IBM machines. Such references simultaneously deny the novel's historical setting, reference the time of its composition, and presage the role of technological invention in the future. For example, during the Avignon briefing, when the diabolically inane Colonel Cathcart orders Major Danby be taken out and shot, a series of unsettling moans causes the briefing room to "[boil] irrepressibly into bedlam" and things like computers to "drop from people's fingers" (231). In this instance Heller imagines a time when computers would be small enough to be held in one's hands. Major Major's seemingly random promotion to major "by an I.B.M. machine" (96) prefigures not only the role computers would play in determining draft lottery numbers during the Vietnam War but also the soldiers' sense of helplessness in face of their unpredictability. The soldier Roger, in David Rabe's *Streamers*, cedes any notion of individual control over to the machines, saying that his deployment is "up to them IBMs. Them machines is figurin' that" (24).

Additionally, certain scenes in *Catch-22* reference topics of civilian social concern emergent in the 1950s and 1960s and hence unrelated to the novel's World War II setting. Principle among these are the intense interrogation scenes featured in chapters 8 and 36, in which Clevinger and Chaplain A. T. Tappman, respectively, find themselves completely cornered and/or outmaneuvered in terrifying ways: both Clevinger and the chaplain end up providing their interrogators the very information needed to convict themselves. Though Heller presents these scenes in his typical "black comedy" style, which makes them read like Laurel and Hardy or Abbott and Costello routines, Clevinger's and the chaplain's attempts to answer to charges leveled against them demonstrate the *likelihood* of a soldier's cracking under interrogation, in this case questioning by his own superiors. Charles S. Young demonstrates not only how civilian concerns over POW interrogation during the Korean War permeated filmic representations of the 1950s and 1960s but also how key films "were forced to flip convention on its head and acknowledge frailty, weakness and unfaithfulness" (2). In declaring that "the wider Korean stalemate . . . threw into question the resolve of the entire nation," Young concludes that "America's inability to prevail was transferred to the prisoners' failure to do the same" (2). Read in this light, Heller's interrogation scenes appear to both reference their contemporaneous counterpart and chide the civilian public for the shifting of blame Young adumbrates. In so doing, *Catch-22* thus features a corrective to civilian understanding of the soldier's experience.

Another corrective for the gap *Male Armor* identifies and investigates arises in Heller's redefinition of heroic masculinity as dereliction of duty—as AWOL masculinity. Heller withholds the nature and details of this redefinition in a manner befitting the narrative style of *Catch-22*. Heller typically introduces skeletal story lines, which tell nearly the complete story, and then returns to them periodically to flesh out details. Some stories are narrated completely only when the reader finishes the novel. Stephen Potts describes Heller's novel as one in which "the reader almost never receives the full text of an episode at its first mention. Characters and scenes recur, and each time they do the narrative adds more information" (28). This technique lends to the novel's pastiche, postmodern feel and its indecipherability yet also serves to tug the inquisitive reader through the intricately interwoven plotlines, for example, the development of Milo Minderbinder's M & M enterprises, the revelation of why Orr began to hold crab apples or horse chestnuts in his cheeks, the explanations for why Orr has a whore beat him over the head with a shoe or even why he crash-lands his plane in the water on every mission. The repeated bits of incidents also eventually flesh out Nately's love affair with his whore, the results of McWatt's bizarre flying practices, the disappearance of Mudd and Clevinger, the appearance of a naked man at Snowden's funeral, and the various and sundry ramifications of the term "catch-22."

In place of linear and chronological plot development, Heller substitutes the ever-increasing number of missions the aircrews are forced to fly, the escalating death toll that eventually wipes out nearly all of Yossarian's friends, and a cumulative heightening of violence. The changes wrought by their war experience manifest in many of the soldiers. Dunbar, for instance, "seldom laughed anymore and seemed to be wasting away. He snarled belligerently at superior officers . . . and was crude and surly and profane even in front of the chaplain" (340). The shifts in Dunbar's behaviors are explained narratively by "the fall in the hospital" that "had either shown him the light or scrambled his brains." Because "it was impossible to say which," Heller here figuratively suggests that the experience of war registers like a blow to the brain (340). Furthermore, Heller alludes to the notion that violence begets violence by coding Dunbar's hostile reactions as enlightenment, a realization that is at once perfectly sensible and completely insane.

Likewise, Yossarian increasingly reacts to his surroundings in a hostile manner. Whereas once he retreated from conflict by entering the hospital, Yossarian begins to respond aggressively by belittling his friends in strings of invectives and wishing or even inflicting ill upon them. Yossarian disdains his role as lead bombardier, and even though having McWatt as a pilot is "one consolation," Yossarian feels he "was still so utterly undefended" (340). Because of this exposure Yossarian "hungered to be demoted again to a wing plane with a loaded machine gun . . . a powerful, heavy, fifty-caliber machine gun he could seize vengefully in both hands and turn loose savagely against all the demons tyrannizing him" (340–41). On the third Thanksgiving recollected in the book, Yossarian indeed does turn a gun on his colleagues. That evening some soldiers frighten Yossarian when in a drunken stupor they accidentally fire their machine guns. Yossarian fires back at them and punches his best friend, Nately, in the nose when Nately tries to stop him. At the height of his own violent episodes, Yossarian seizes McWatt by the throat and threatens to strangle him for his frenetic flying methods.

The culmination of this trajectory of increasing violence occurs in chapter 39, entitled "The Eternal City." In this chapter Yossarian goes AWOL in Rome and witnesses various forms of brutality being inflicted upon the weak: dogs, children, and women. In each scene, narrated in surreal fashion, representatives of military or police law fail to protect the innocent, or worse, perpetrate the crimes. Yossarian's witnessing of these events signifies not only the inefficacy of the systems meant to prevent atrocity but also the devastating effects of war on noncombatants. As a retreat Yossarian ducks into the private apartments kept for soldiers on leave, only to find that his compatriot Aarfy has just hurled a prostitute named Michaela out the window to her death. Aside from the military commanders, who place advancing their careers over the security of the men under their auspices, Aarfy remains the only character resolutely unaffected by the novel's violence. Aarfy's nonchalance, despite Yossarian's protest that he "murdered a human being" (428), instantiates how wartime acceptance of brutality and killing permeates the entire culture and disrupts standards of moral action.

Moreover, Michaela's murder creates a situation that virtually guarantees readerly condemnation of Aarfy's act. In *Writing War in the Twentieth Century* Margot Norris stunningly analyzes a similar scene of moral repugnance in interpreting Ernest Hemingway's *A Farewell to Arms*. Observing that Frederic Henry "kills (or partially kills) only one man—the Italian sergeant who refuses to help him move his truck"—Norris claims that "the novel's narration of that act makes it very clear that this particular war casualty is produced by an act of cold-blooded murder" (63). Noting "readerly resistance to accepting this point (and its larger ramification, that the violence of war permits and produces many such murders)" (64), Norris reads Hemingway's refusal to change the scene as "an act of narrative aggression," which she summarizes as "a willingness to frustrate and disappoint readers by telling them not what they want to hear but what they don't want to hear" (64). Likewise, for readers of *Catch-22* the scene of Michaela's murder lurches from the novel's pages as almost too morbid, given the novel's predominantly comic tone.

I would like to suggest, however, that like Hemingway, Heller desires the audience's resistance to and condemnation of Aarfy's act, for he resolves the scene by having the military police who arrive at the scene arrest Yossarian for being AWOL. During the prolonged period of wailing sirens while readers await the police's arrival, however, the expectation is that justice will prevail for Michaela and that Aarfy will at long last get his due. But when the police take Yossarian away, and not Aarfy, Heller begins his attempt to bridge the gap between civilian understanding and soldierly experience. He does so by following Michaela's murder almost immediately with the fullest exposition of perhaps the most tantalizingly suspended and emotionally significant of the cumulative narrative stories in the novel: the death of Snowden. In the novel's penultimate chapter, "Snowden," readers at long last learn not only how Snowden dies but also his secret, to which Yossarian repeatedly alludes, and Heller thus seems to ask that his readers extend the same repugnance for Snowden's death as they readily do for the death of innocent Michaela.

Snowden's death is not coded with such awesome significance when the reader first learns of it, during one of Clevinger's "education sessions" that Yossarian attends in Captain Black's tent. Yossarian asks, to the horror of his classmates, "Where are the Snowdens of yesteryear?" (44). The classmates know that "Snowden had been killed over Avignon when Dobbs went crazy in mid-air and seized the controls away from Huple," but none of them dare remind Yossarian of that fact, as the memory tends to make Yossarian rather crazy. Yossarian again mentions Snowden when he briefly recalls the mission to Avignon and remembers that "Snowden lay dying in back" (59). The most complete narration of the events surrounding Snowden's death before chapter 41 occurs when the novel revisits Yossarian's hospital stay, which also opens the book. Yossarian reflects that "being in the hospital was better than being over Bologna or flying over Avignon with Huple and Dobbs at the controls and Snowden dying in back" (175).

During this recollection Yossarian also first refers to Snowden's secret, remembering that "Snowden had frozen to death after spilling his secret to Yossarian in the back of the plane" (176). At this revelation the repetition of the sentences "I'm cold. I'm cold" throughout the text takes on a haunting, somber note. On page 182 Yossarian offers his first rendition of the secret: "They were out to get him." Ostensibly, then, the secret is that the ever-nebulous "they" were out to "get" Yossarian, and "Snowden had spilled it all over the back of the plane" (182). Perhaps this portent of imminent demise provokes Yossarian's next recollection of Snowden, when Yossarian attempts to place blame for his not wanting to fly any more missions. Evoking the mission to Avignon once again, Heller writes, "That was the mission on which Yossarian lost his nerve. Yossarian lost his nerve on the mission to

Avignon because Snowden lost his guts, and Snowden lost his guts because their pilot that day was Huple, who was only fifteen years old, and their co-pilot was Dobbs, who was even worse and who wanted Yossarian to join with him in a plot to murder Colonel Cathcart" (235). By placing the blame for his loss of nerve on the death of Snowden, Yossarian subordinates nearly every other narrative thread of the novel to the development of this one involving Snowden's death, for if one thing characterizes Yossarian throughout the text more than any other, it is his persistent desire to be grounded from flying missions or to get out of the war completely.

In several pages of intense dramatic exposition, the full narration of Snowden's death finally occurs in Snowden's self-titled chapter. Heller describes in acute detail how Snowden's guts slither out across the floor of the airplane when Yossarian removes Snowden's flak jacket and discovers the shrapnel wound Snowden has sustained. Yossarian's ignominious attempts to stave the flow of life from Snowden's body fail. Because of the prior references to Snowden "spilling" his secret, the reader initially thinks that the secret consists of his guts. However, the sight of viscera on the floor prompts Yossarian to reveal that Snowden's "secret" consists of words: "Man was matter. . . . Drop him out a window and he'll fall. Set fire to him and he'll burn. Bury him and he'll rot like other kinds of garbage. The spirit gone, man is garbage" (450).

Given this event's relatively early occurrence in the novel's *chronology*, Yossarian's refusal either to lose his spirit (or his life) in the insanity of war or to be treated as matter by the military retroactively enables the reader to view him as heroic, instead of as a whining soldier who shirks his duty. The rather late *narration* of this event, however, serves to superimpose the reader's exoneration of Yossarian's actions onto Yossarian's decision to go AWOL. The result is the reader's sympathetic association with a character who denies traditional notions of soldierly masculinity. Yossarian remains the same character who insists to Major Major, unheroically, that "there are ten million men in uniform who could replace me. Some people are getting killed and a lot more are making money and having fun. Let somebody else get killed" (113). But as the novel climaxes, he becomes morally justified in this earlier demurring—Yossarian's escape at novel's end, despite any questions about loyalty or duty that it may raise, emerges as the *only* appropriate response to his catch-22. Hence, Heller effectively rescripts World War II heroic masculinity as a dereliction of military duty and establishes a trope of unheroic soldierly masculinity that will reappear in later representations of war, such as Tim O'Brien's *The Things They Carried* and David O. Russell's *Three Kings,* among others. O'Brien's self-named speaker, in the section of his novel entitled "On the Rainy River," says, "I was a coward. I went to the war" (61), while Russell's four principal "Kings" go AWOL to achieve their stature.[1]

Yossarian's interpretation of Snowden's secret also suggests the status of heroic masculinity in Cold War culture, a status that harkens back to early and forward to late twentieth-century definitions of manhood in American culture. Heller insists that the horrors of war cannot sustain the ideals of courage, bravery, and heroism attendant upon traditional definitions of masculinity, and in that way he models Hemingway's presentation of World War I veterans in *In Our Time, The Sun Also Rises,* and *A Farewell to Arms.* Rather than making men, Heller declares, war only suffices to unmake them. In dramatizing this unmaking through the violent dissolution of the soldierly body—literally spilling his guts out—Heller unwittingly presages an image of threatened masculinity that would come to dominate representations of the Vietnam War: the male body in pieces. In the handful of years after *Catch-22*'s publication, as Americans witnessed their country's increasing investment in Southeast Asia and eventual war with North Vietnam, many of the novel's idiosyncratic characteristics would also seem to describe the experiences of soldiers deployed to keep the dominoes from tumbling in America's most prolonged Cold War–era hot war.[2]

# CHAPTER 3

# ENVELOPE, PLEASE

*The Metonymic Male*

## Unit Cohesion, Bodily Coherence, and the Vietnam War

At one point in *Dispatches,* Michael Herr's memoir of the years he spent in Vietnam as a correspondent for *Esquire* magazine, Herr calls *Catch-22* "a Nam standard because it said that in a war everybody thinks that everybody else is crazy" (210). While *Catch-22* repeatedly features the idea that war makes everyone crazy, Herr's summation glosses a number of other reasons for *Catch-22*'s status as a "Nam standard," including its fragmented, chaotic narration; its portrayal of the absolute inanity of organizational structures like the military or capitalism; its depiction of the careerism of military leaders and their near-total disconnection from realities on the ground; and its revelation of the insignificance of what were once regarded as heroic, manly behaviors. In addition to these characteristics, this chapter explains the grunts' fascination with *Catch-22* using the image of Snowden's guts slithering across the floor of the damaged airplane and the attendant, repulsive "secret" that Yossarian translates: "Man was matter. . . . Drop him out a window and he'll fall. Set fire to him and he'll burn. Bury him and he'll rot like other kinds of garbage. The spirit gone, man is garbage" (Heller 450). In other words, I argue that *Catch-22* became a "Nam standard" because in the scene of Snowden's evisceration, grunts recognized both their sense of their own irrelevance and the dire necessity of keeping their bodies intact.

The image of Snowden's dissolution obtained its immense signification because the military used body counts, instead of traditional battles over territory, to measure victory during the Vietnam War. In *The Remasculinization of America* Susan Jeffords describes how the body, because it was used to determine victory, came to be metonymically represented through its constituent parts. Jeffords records that "anything counted as a body— arm, leg, torso" (7). While Jeffords uses these details to discuss the importance performance plays in representations of Vietnam, this chapter interrogates how the metonymic function of body parts creates an atmosphere in which the fragmented body signifies falsely, or more likely fails to signify altogether, especially in terms of victory. Fragmented bodies, even when called to do so, cannot represent victory, and they are, therefore, metaphorical for a victory that finally was not forthcoming. Implicated in the idea of victory is America's entire justification for fighting the war in the first place—defense of the nation, and subsequently of the world, against Communist aggression abroad—and the validation of conceptions of American masculinity at home.

Representations of the Vietnam War, including Herr's memoir *Dispatches* and David Rabe's play *Streamers,* replicate Yossarian's repugnance for the myriad ways bodies can fall apart. In my reading of these texts, aspects of the seemingly "different" style of war Vietnam necessitated combine in *Dispatches* and *Streamers* to force the individual soldier to focus on the maintenance of his own bodily coherence rather than on the attainment of a collective victory. These "differences" include the twelve-month tour of duty; the presence of the media; racial integration of combat troops; and altered military tactics, including shifts from "traditional" to "guerilla" strategies.[1]

Concerns for bodily coherence over collective victory litter *Dispatches* and *Streamers.* For example, Herr describes "blindness, loss of legs, arms or balls, major and lasting disfigurement" (14), and Rabe's play opens with Martin's attempted suicide. Richie wishes to conceal Martin's slashed wrists so military officials will not perceive Martin as a coward for his desire to escape service. Herr's fear of disfigurement and Richie's shame over Martin's actions accentuate how even non-life-threatening injuries take on special significance in representations of the Vietnam War. This chapter demonstrates that when the United States structured victory around intact male bodies—ours hold together, the enemy's do not—soldierly investment in the intact male body reaffirmed American society's investment in a nation-defining masculinity, intent on the cohesion of men's bodies. Thus, the inviolate male body became symbol and guarantor not only of victory and masculinity but also of the manner in which Americans viewed themselves. This chapter reads intimations of homosexuality and the difficulties of integration of the troops as metaphorical threats to the coherence of the male body and suggests that the threats presented by sexual and racial difference provided ready civilian access to the significance of bodily and unit cohesion during the Southeast Asian conflict. The gap between civilian understanding and soldierly experience at the center of *Male Armor*'s study thus emerges during Vietnam in the conflict between the civilian expectations of victory—that is, that the male body and the combat unit will cohere—and the soldierly experience that, indeed, they cannot. This experience paradoxically reduces the soldier's investment in civilian ideals of masculinity by linking cohesion to survival instead of to victory. If the difficulties faced by returning Vietnam veterans stand as any testament, the gap between civilian and soldierly definitions of masculinity may never have been so broad or so entrenched.

The conflict in Vietnam extended the United States' policy for containing the spread of Communism—first executed during the Korean War—and tested not only America's self-view but also the nation's appetite for war and its traditional execution of war. The first major variation between the military's conduct of the Vietnam War and its conduct of previous wars emerged in the implementation of a twelve-month tour of duty, first experimented with during the Korean War. (Marine Corps members served thirteen months.) Military officials hoped that by limiting the length of a tour they could exponentially increase soldierly productivity, commitment, and morale, while fostering the same at home.

Quite possibly, the opposite proved true. As Susan Jeffords notes in her study of representations of Vietnam, *The Remasculinization of America,* "the 365-day calendars handed out by the Red Cross emphasized the extent to which the individual soldier's perception of the war was focused on the immediate survival of a given number of days rather than on 'winning' the war" (7). Moreover, instead of increasing public support for the war, the foreshortened term may have had a negative impact in this sphere as well, as many of the soldiers returned home to join protestors in criticizing American goals or the likelihood of their achievement. As Terry Anderson notes, "Unlike fathers coming home after World War II, Vietnam veterans rarely talked of heroism, duty, honor. Instead, the 'endless war' became an endless barrage of horror stories and disillusionment" (247). Anderson argues that returning veterans testified to the war's violence and brutality, even if they did not participate in political or social protest.

And returning veterans were not the only ones to raise concerns over the war's brutality. The media also criticized the violence of the war, the government's handling of it, and the likelihood of an American victory. For the first time in any war era, the media in Vietnam included television. Because popular support for the war continued nearly until its completion, many critics have argued that television portrayal of images from the war had no ill effect on public perception, at least not an empirically demonstrable one. Demands for empirical proof, however, elide both the immediacy and the omnipresence of television images and the fact that such images comprised an altogether different experience of war for home-front Americans.

Analysts agree, for the most part, upon television's restrained portrayal of atrocities in Vietnam. George Roeder, for instance, claims that media representations of the Vietnam conflict, though free from the censorial restraints implemented during World War II, nevertheless evidenced an escalation in the depiction of violence as the war progressed. Roeder claims that "as in World War II, sufferings caused by and inflicted on the enemy were shown earlier and in greater detail" and that "the longer the conflict continued, the more revealing the imagery became" (131). Chester J. Pach Jr. contends that "about half of the film reports on network newscasts concerned U.S. troops on foot or in helicopters searching out the enemy, exchanging fire with snipers, calling in air strikes on base camps and supply depots, or clearing guerrillas from hostile villages" (94). These reports thus "showed the war as it was—a confused, fragmented, and questionable endeavor" (Pach 91). Both Roeder and Pach anxiously uphold television's self-adjudicated reticence to portray grotesque images of American dead. Pach says that "editors hardly ever allowed ghastly pictures of the dead or dying into American homes during the dinner hour" (95). Similarly, Roeder states that "during the war network executives . . . never showed American soldiers with brains or intestines oozing out, or anyone who had just issued himself a reprieve from combat by shooting off his foot, or the mutilated body of a Vietnamese rape victim" (136).

Roeder defends the American media's restraint by labeling as vapid "claims that television brought home to viewers the full reality of war" (136). Roeder admits, however, that certain television stories were critical of governmental and military operation of the war, some emerging rather early in the conflict. For instance, Roeder cites a 1965 story by Morley Safer that detailed "the American burning of the village of Cam Ne," claiming that it "differed significantly from anything shown during World War II" and that it "must have provoked doubts about U.S. policy in the minds of many viewers" (135). In the same vein Pach notes that "during 1967 network newscasts contained stronger and more frequent criticism of American methods of warfare" (105). Pach concludes that "nightly news coverage did contribute to popular dissatisfaction with the war" (112).

For veterans returning from the war, the effect of television's nightly news emerged quite clearly. In the collection *Why Vietnam Still Matters,* compiled in honor of the dedication of the Vietnam Veterans Memorial in Washington, D.C., Shad Meshad writes: "Media coverage put the combat servicemen in the spotlight, portraying them as perpetrators of death and destruction, unlike the noble heroes of past wars. The Vietnam servicemen and women, like all who had served before them, risked their lives on a daily and hourly basis to ensure freedom for those who waited at home. Yet, the Vietnam veteran came home to criticism and blame for being part of this vastly unpopular war, through no fault of their own" (66). While Meshad would like to believe that veterans were implicated through "no fault of their own," the media simultaneously broadcast the activities of war protestors and draft dodgers, thus introducing the possibility that veterans could have also avoided service. Still, Meshad's belief reflects an understandable overexaggeration of the effects of media coverage of the war. Even the war's status as "vastly unpopular" is not supported by public opinion polls until nearly the end of the crisis. Regardless of his reasons for participating, any soldier returning from the conflict who experienced the rejection faced by many Vietnam veterans rightfully indulged in justification of that rejection—in this case by blaming the media.

But Meshad does emphasize some of the means through which the media's role in Vietnam altered American experience of geopolitical upheaval.

Imagistically, the Vietnam conflict did not lend itself to the same manner of depiction previous wars had. As Roeder notes, no maps showing territory lost and/or gained were shown to the American public, as they had been in the World Wars; this is how body counts of enemy dead came to stand in for territorial gains and hence for victory (Roeder 132). While the military and the government hoped such reports would lend to home-front support of the war effort, they instead fomented negative images of the soldiers sent to do their country's "duty," effectively preventing the returning veterans' hero status and circumventing public perception of war's honorable purpose. As one soldier in *Dispatches* remarks, "We're here to kill gooks. Period" (20). Americans thus received the message that soldiers were killing machines, and when body counts finally did not equal victory, the killing emerged as violence for its own sake. Conceived of hence as brutalizers, soldiers felt directly the gap between civilian understanding and their own experience. Quite simply, they earned no reward for upholding the American and masculinist ideals they had purportedly gone to war to validate.

As demonstrated throughout *Male Armor,* the connection between masculine validation and military engagement, the former dependent upon the latter, has a long and convoluted history in the United States. The conflict in Vietnam, no less than its predecessors, also registered the possibility of masculine attainment or validation. Christian Appy claims that "the celebrations of military culture so central to many World War II movies and enacted in childhood games undoubtedly played an important role in shaping a glorified view of war among many young boys of the Vietnam generation" (61). In other words, despite all Cold War conformist culture had done to challenge notions of heroic masculinity, despite *Catch-22* and other literary assessments of war, boys coming of age in the 1960s still clung to vagaries of heroic masculinity attainable through war.

The African American soldiers chronicled in Wallace Terry's collection *Bloods* repeatedly invoke manhood as the reward of war experience, if not as the primary reason for participation. Their full integration into combat troops for the first time in the Vietnam War appeared to offer a golden opportunity for their ability to signify as men, an ability hitherto largely denied by American culture at large. Stephen A. Howard's mother assures him that he'll "be back a man" (Terry 118); Robert A. Daniels goes to war because he "didn't have anybody to sort of rear [him] into becomin' a man" (230); and "Gene" Woodley Jr., while in Vietnam, "collected about 14 ears and fingers" as "a symbol of combat-type manhood" (244).

Woodley's use of body-part trophies to demonstrate manhood adroitly summarizes the brand of soldierly masculinity emergent in Vietnam for all U.S. soldiers of any race. I would like to suggest that this new form of manhood, influenced by the new tour of duty, resulted from the war's emphasis on body counts and refashioned the soldier-hero's altruistic focus on the group to a singular focus on his own bodily coherence. Naturally, then, this focus on bodily coherence also informed definitions of masculinity in American culture and emerges in the literature of the Vietnam era.

Kaja Silverman addresses the coherence of the male body in her book *Male Subjectivity at the Margins,* in which she claims that masculinity is "necessarily fortified against any knowledge of the void upon which it rests, and—as its insistence upon an unimpaired bodily 'envelope' would suggest— fiercely protective of its coherence" (63). Silverman calls the belief system or ideological structure at work fortifying masculinity, "against any knowledge of the void upon which it rests," the Dominant Fiction, and she claims that this fiction resides in what she calls the American "cultural imaginary." The Dominant Fiction, she asserts, holds the coherence of the male body as a precondition of the structure's continuing function. In explaining the existence and function of the Dominant Fiction, Silverman says that it "consists of the images and stories through which a society figures consensus; images and stories which cinema, fiction, popular culture, and other forms of mass representation presumably both draw upon and help to shape" (30). Michael Herr, calling aspects of this Dominant Fiction "mythic tracks," includes "the lowest John Wayne wetdream" and "the most aggravated soldier-poet fantasy" (20) among the soldiers' motivations for going to war.

The Dominant Fiction, according to Silverman, "forms the stable core around which a nation's and a period's 'reality' coheres" (*Male Subjectivity* 41). Because her theory links ideology and male subjectivity in a dependent binary, Silverman argues that any rupture within this system, created by an injury to the male bodies signifying it, impedes and sometimes prevents its maintenance. When Yossarian witnesses Snowden's guts trailing across the floor of the airplane, his belief in the inviolability of man disintegrates, and he no longer wishes to participate in war. Yossarian experiences what Silverman describes as a "traumatic encounter with lack," which often registers as the "impairment of [a male subject's] anatomical masculinity" (62). Yossarian proceeds to remove his bloodstained uniform and lingers about base camp completely naked, his nakedness testifying as much to his bodily coherence, and hence to his manhood, as to his ideological protest.

While physical wounds lurk as possible impairments in *Dispatches* and *Streamers,* yet another rupture to the binary linking ideology and male subjectivity emerges in the texts through intimations of homosexuality. The Dominant Fiction, which "offers the representational system by means of which the subject typically assumes a sexual identity" (Silverman, *Male Subjectivity* 41), defines homosexuality through acts that identify its practitioners, chiefly anal penetration. Likewise, D. A. Miller classifies the anus as "the popularly privileged site of gay male sex, the orifice whose sexual use general opinion considers the least dispensable element in defining the true homosexual" (134). This connection in popular opinion between homosexual identity and bodily penetration also entails that society cannot view the homosexual as a man. As David Buchbinder claims, "Prohibited . . . from even being thought of in the dominant (and therefore heterosexual) discourse of masculinity is the idea that the male body too can be erotically or sexually penetrated" (44). Therefore, the intimation of homosexuality, like the threat of injury, introduces possible ruptures to the male body and, as the male body serves as guarantor of the Dominant Fiction in Silverman's elaboration, to the Dominant Fiction itself.

Because it occurs in an all-male arena, war represents an anticipatory landscape of heightened threats of homosexuality and hence a testing ground for masculinity and the Dominant Fiction. In his book *What a Man's Gotta Do,* Antony Easthope claims that "at present masculinity is defined mainly in the way an individual deals with his femininity and his desire for other men" (6). According to Easthope, men respond to this desire through a process of sublimation, which Easthope finds "fundamental to the social order, transforming unacceptable sexual drive into something more conventional." Easthope claims that in the social order "desexualized, sublimated love for other men becomes available to form the male bond, enabling men to work together for each other" (15).

Despite sublimation and the male bonds forged through shared work, in *Dispatches* and *Streamers* homosexuality emerges in the anticipation of injuries, which are used to represent homosexuality metaphorically. When she claims, in *The Body in Pain,* that "the anticipatory injury is an actual injury" (79), Elaine Scarry describes the manner in which heterosexual servicemembers experience the homosexuality of their peers. The elision between actual and imagined injury entails that the literal rupture of the male body through anal penetration (i.e., "actual" homosexuality) parallels the rupture the mere presence of homosexuals in the armed forces precipitates (i.e., "anticipatory" homosexuality) and suffices to dismantle "unit cohesion." Though *Dispatches* rarely discusses homosexuality explicitly, Herr's characterization of war machinery and technology as sexual means that actions associated with the machinery emerge as sexualized. Additionally, homoerotic desire lurks everywhere in the attention Herr pays to his reminiscences. David Rabe, on the other hand, openly confronts homosexuality as a threat to the masculine arena extant in the military. Like Scarry, Herr's text makes no distinction between a threatened injury and an actual one. In Rabe's play, however, no threat to masculinity or to the Dominant Fiction emerges until after an actual injury has occurred. In both *Dispatches* and *Streamers* the metaphoric representation of homosexuality through threatened or actual wounds to the male body serves to uphold masculinity by emerging as something to be sublimated, something to be kept from impeding a masculinity signified by the intact male body.

## Upholding Masculinity: Homoerotic Desire, Racially Integrated Units, and the Masculine Collective

For some reason, when William Broyles Jr. admits of the Vietnam War that "I miss it because I loved it, loved it in strange and troubling ways" (56), his confession reads much less apologetically than Michael Herr's "I'd loved it there too" (251). Perhaps one reads apology in Herr's statement because it comes near the end of more than 250 pages that are seemingly more about the conflict than Herr's response to it, or because the statement follows shortly upon Herr's admission that in Vietnam he'd "performed half an act" (251). Regardless of its inflection, Herr's desire to group himself with others who loved Vietnam belies his need to establish his "being there" as authentic.

In her analysis of *Dispatches,* in *The Remasculinization of America,* Susan Jeffords engages Michael Herr's need to establish his presence in Vietnam and therefore his ability to accurately write about the war. Jeffords categorizes Herr's book as a personal experience narrative, a documentary form that alienates those who did not participate. This classification echoes William Broyles Jr.'s statement that the purpose of Vietnam narratives is "not to enlighten, but exclude" (61), and reflects the common sentiment that "being there" entails combat service. Herr's account, Jeffords claims, tracks his movement from a position of exclusion to a place within what Jeffords terms the "male collective," where soldiers "successfully [eliminate] hierarchical difference by subordinating it to the broader value system of 'survival'" (54). The military relies upon the disavowal of difference Jeffords describes to create unit cohesion. Jeffords classifies Herr's position outside as a feminine one and his entry into the collective as his masculinization.[2]

While Jeffords's demarcation between feminine and masculine subject positions proves useful in analyzing the text, the idea that Herr makes a demonstrable and irretractable move from one gender position to another deserves reconsideration. Jeffords's reading *can* be easily plotted through the text. Herr admits within the first couple of pages that he was not "ready for this" (5) and shortly thereafter that he "never belonged" (10) in the jungle. Later, Herr recounts "developing a real war metabolism," one in which "you slow yourself down when your heart tried to punch its way through your chest" (14), which indicates the nascent stages of his movement into the male collective Jeffords theorizes. Herr later claims that "it took me a month to lose that feeling of being a spectator to something that was part game, part show" (168), which seems to describe Jeffords's move from exterior to interior, until one notes that Herr has presaged this statement more than a hundred pages earlier with the memory that "after a year I felt so plugged in" (31). So Herr's traverse from a feminine subject position outside to a masculine one inside at one point takes but a month yet at another requires a year?

I compare these quotations to demonstrate the difficulty of plotting Herr's disjointed text on the developmental model Jeffords posits. But other aspects of *Dispatches* prohibit any belief that Herr came to occupy a determined and static space within the male collective. In fact, in his recollection of the days prior to his departure from Vietnam, Herr articulates the palpable hatred many of the grunts directed toward members of the press corps: "We were called thrill freaks, death-wishers, wound-seekers, war-lovers, hero-worshippers, closet queens, dope addicts, low-grade alcoholics, ghouls, communists, seditionists, more nasty things than I can remember" (228). Herr's use of the plural "we" indicates his presence among the press corps, a presence categorically outside the male collective. Furthermore, Herr earlier recounts an individual experience of his alien status, saying the grunts "only hated me, hated me the way you'd hate any hopeless fool who would put himself through this thing when he had choices, any fool who had no more need of his life than to play with it in this way" (208). The grunts who feel these emotions are the very same "death-spaced grunts" who are "so nonchalant about the horror and fear that you knew you'd never really be one of them no matter how long you stayed" (235). Quite possibly, Herr's memoir reads apologetically because what he most desired was to be "one of them," so at the very least his narrative position oscillates between inclusion and exclusion. When toward the end of his memoirs he claims that he "was in many ways brother to these poor, tired grunts" (206), the ways in which he is not brother beg investigation.

Upon closer scrutiny, a sense that Herr's identity as a war correspondent places him unequivocally outside the male collective in fact pervades Herr's text, and Herr's cognizance of this fact necessitates his push to justify his being there. Evidence of the correspondent's remove from the grunts emerges in the motility Herr cherishes—"we could have choppers like taxis" (8)—which often allows him to choose whether he remains in an area or not, a choice denied the grunts who people his reminiscences. He need only shout, "Bao Chi! Bao Chi!" (231), the Vietnamese words for journalist, and in most cases he will not be shot at—the words performatively constituting those who iterate them as noncombative and therefore distinguished from the soldiers. In fact, Herr recounts incidents when his presence was uncomfortable for the men with whom he claims to have been so intimate. He relates how the grunts "didn't always know what to think about you or what to say to you, they'd sometimes call you 'Sir' until you had to beg them to stop" (206). Furthermore, whenever Herr moves to a different location, the soldiers in the bunkers feel ill at ease "lying around with a stranger" (186), so his nomadic nature thus also keeps him from becoming a part of the male collective.

Herr also figures as outside the male collective in his interactions with black soldiers in Vietnam. As Jeffords delineates it, the male collective constitutes a place where soldiers "successfully eliminated hierarchical difference by subordinating it to the broader value system of 'survival'" (54). Some of the black veterans included in Terry's collection claim to have attained such equanimity, at least among combatant units. Harold "Light Bulb" Bryant recalls that "we didn't have racial incidents like what was happening in the rear area, 'cause we had to depend on each other. We were always in the bush" (23). Another combatant, Arthur E. "Gene" Woodley Jr., calls a fellow white soldier "brother" "because in a war circumstance, we all brothers"

(242). These veterans assent to both their individual and their collective unit's denial of racial difference in service of survival—that is, the successful rendering of the male collective.

Herr, on the other hand, continually, if inadvertently, focuses upon the difference between himself and the African American soldiers he recollects. For instance, Herr recalls the "black staff sergeant in the Cav who had taken [Herr] over to his outfit for dinner the night before" but, upon hearing the news of Martin Luther King Jr.'s assassination on 4 April 1968, had "cut [Herr] dead." When this staff sergeant comes "to the press tent later that night" and voices his concern over how to pursue a military career when the government may ask him to "turn them guns around on [his] own people," Herr says, "What can I tell you?" (158–59). Similarly, when Herr encounters the "really big spade, rough-looking even when he smiled," who wears a "gold nose-bead fastened through his left nostril," each man attempts to get a rise out of the other—the soldier by claiming he's a Black Panther sent to recruit in Vietnam and Herr by calmly asserting he has met Panthers before. The Panther then retracts his claim of membership. As he is choppered out of the area, however, the soldier gives Herr "the sign" (181), and Herr emerges as duped. As with the staff sergeant to whom Herr had nothing to say, little communication occurs between Herr and this grunt, even though they "talked for an hour" and the Panther "laid a joint on" Herr (180). The differences between Herr and these men are not subsumed enough that communication can occur between them.

Differences also emerge between Herr and other African American grunts he recalls, differences that replicate hierarchies of race supposedly outmoded by troop integration and within the masculine collective as well. These differences occur because Herr typically equates black soldiers with traditionally feminine subject positions. Aside from the two recollections detailed above, in eleven of the thirteen other incidents including African American characters, Herr associates the soldiers with either music or a feminized nurturing position. Herr recalls how African American marines on leave would spend more time around "the best jukebox in Vietnam" than on China Beach. Herr first hears Jimi Hendrix, for instance, when he seeks cover from enemy fire in a rice paddy. A chopper rises out of the paddy carrying a "grinning black corporal hunched over a cassette recorder" (181), from which the Hendrix issues. Additionally, Herr recalls a black soldier called Bu Dop (177); one with the Ninth Division called the Entertainer

(251); and one who has taken the title of a Supremes single, Love Child, as his Vietnam moniker (190). Ostensibly, these recollections associate blacks with rock and roll, the soundtrack for Vietnam, but two of them also connect the black men with feminine subject positions, notably Love Child, with his choice of a female group's song title, and the black corporal who plays Hendrix. Herr claims that "the Airborne in Vietnam was full of wiggy-brilliant spades like [the corporal], really mean and really good, *guys who always took care of you when things got bad*" (181, emphasis added).

Herr's description of these "wiggy-brilliant spades" and their caring role highlights the near uniformity of the role Herr assigns to African American soldiers. For instance, Herr hears about a black marine who, during the "heavy shelling at Con Thien," had reassured fellow soldiers, saying, "Don't worry, baby, God'll think of something" (56–57). The marine called Philly Dog also provides reassurance, because he is "about the only man in Delta Company who hadn't been hurt yet" (73).[3] When Herr disembarks from a chopper at full run in order to avoid being hit by enemy incoming, a black marine assures him that there "ain' no hurry-up no more" (162). Each of these men exhibits a feminine quality of reassurance, as, at least in Herr's recollection, they coddle the journalist in mothering, protective ways.

Several other black soldiers operate in similar fashion both toward Herr and toward fellow grunts. On Herr's first afternoon in country, an African American sergeant attempts to keep Herr from boarding a Chinook headed for heavy fighting by telling him he is "too new to go near the kind of shit they were throwing around up in those hills" (168). When a mad Vietnamese boy enters the streets near the Citadel, Herr recalls a black soldier running to rescue the boy. The soldier comforts the boy by saying, "C'mon, poor li'l baby, 'fore one a these grunt mothers shoots you," and "carrie[s] the boy to where the corpsmen were" (79). And finally, Herr also classifies Day Tripper, Mayhew's black friend, as a caretaker. Day Tripper faults Mayhew's decision to reenlist and insists that Mayhew remain in the bunker for protection during incoming shelling.

Theoretical discussions of African American male subjectivity posit that such characterizations denigrate the black soldiers. In *Heavenly Bodies* Richard Dyer contends that "the treatment of black men . . . constantly puts them into 'feminine' positions that place them structurally . . . in the same positions as women typically occupy" (116–17). Herr positions the African American soldiers he recollects in feminine mothering roles and hence relocates discussions of their subjectivity from realms of race to those of gender. Robyn Wiegman theorizes this shift thus: "The African-American male's inclusion in the separate world of the masculine is accomplished by detaching him from the historical context of race and installing him instead within the framework of gender. Here, the homosocial bond's assertion of a stridently undifferentiated masculine space can function to veil its simultaneous rejuvenation of racial hierarchies" (125). So while integration putatively endows black men with masculinity by enabling their participation in the homosocial bond, the organization of black men into feminine representational roles reinvents their subordination to white men. This subordination exists within the supposedly coequal collective and, in this case, even though he seems appreciative of their efforts, is also present for Herr.

Herr's own feminized subject position, from which he desires rescue, necessitates this reinscription of racial hierarchies. Herr's attempt to repudiate this position emerges with Tim Page's claim that he and Herr are "not men," but instead "correspondents" (7). Though Page means to suggest that the members of the press are not *among* the men, meaning the fighting men, the statement holds in Page's indelibly comic style the double entendre of their being anatomically not men as well. Jeffords notes this inference from the Fourth Division LURP soldier on his third tour of Vietnam, who classifies the press as "tits on a bull" (Herr 6). Though the soldier undoubtedly utilizes the idiom for its suggestion of superfluity, Jeffords reads the phrase as a mark of gender for members of the press (42), a mark Herr also understands. His narrative, inflected with this judgment of his femininity and uselessness, serves as a means to combat the designation.

The "tits on a bull" classification centers upon press members' noncombatant status, the fact that they do not possess guns, which symbolize phallic power and represent the phallus. Since Herr does not utilize a gun, and cannot therefore put himself in the grunts' place (Herr 31), he serves as a castrated figure, one without the phallus. Kaja Silverman's conception of the Dominant Fiction rests upon the commensurability of the penis and the phallus (15). In Silverman's system, then, Herr emerges as a doubly castrated figure. He has no weapon, and he becomes the male subject who experiences trauma as an "impairment of his anatomical masculinity" (Silverman 62). Herr attempts to recuperate at least one level of this castration using his pen, hence his justificatory stance for "being there." The pen, finally, does not measure up to the gun or the phallus, and references to anatomical damage litter Herr's account in an almost obsessive manner. For example, Herr recalls a new press agent who asks about *The Wound*—"What does it look like when a man gets hit in the balls?" (133)—and he indicates that this was the question the new agent had "really meant to ask all along" (38).

Mirroring Elaine Scarry's claim that the anticipated wound constitutes an actual one, Herr seems to fear the *possibility* of a wound as much as what it might *actually do* to his bodily envelope. He says, "You could be in the most protected space in Vietnam and still know that your safety was provisional, that early death, blindness, loss of legs, arms or balls, major and lasting disfigurement . . . could come in on the freakyfluky as easily as in the so-called expected ways" (14). The reiteration of this fear supports Jeffords's claim that Herr enters the male collective by facing the same "traumatic encounters with lack" faced by the grunts. For Herr death is the great equalizer, to whom it does not "matter that you were young and had plans, that you were loved, that you were a noncombatant, an observer" (135). However, in "Colleagues," when digressing about the number of correspondents killed in Vietnam (230–33), Herr attempts to equate his experience with that of the grunts, even though shortly thereafter he refers to these same grunts as the aforementioned "death-spaced," with whom the correspondents will never be one. Herr implicitly recognizes the correspondents' position outside the grunts' masculine collective, despite their witnessing of the same events.

Herr pursues entry into the male collective by writing *Dispatches*, because, as he says, those who "can't find [their] courage in a war . . . have to keep looking for it anyway" (259). His writing, then, represents his "denial of castration," upon which, according to Silverman, "classic male subjectivity" rests (44). Herr acknowledges his own lack of courage in facing the war when he recollects "years of thinking this or that about what happens to you when you pursue a fantasy until it becomes experience, and then afterward you can't handle the experience" (68). At another point he says that "I went to cover the war, and the war covered me" (20).

Herr's inability to countenance his own cowardice, even years after the war, emerges as a sort of "war neurosis." In her summary of Freud's *Beyond the Pleasure Principle*, Silverman claims that Freud infers that "the subject suffering from a war neurosis constantly relives his traumatic experiences as a way of binding those experiences, and so of integrating them harmoniously into his psychic organization" (56). Herr writes to deny his castration, his uselessness; he writes to justify his presence within the male collective;

he writes because he has the pen instead of the gun as phallus. Each reason suggests an attempt to justify his masculinity. The writing of *Dispatches,* then, becomes Herr's means of mastery over his war neurosis and his feelings of castration, poignantly articulated through the repetition "Vietnam Vietnam Vietnam": "After enough time passed and memory receded and settled, the name itself became a prayer, coded like all prayer to go past the extremes of petition and gratitude: Vietnam Vietnam Vietnam, say again, until the word lost all its old loads of pain, pleasure, horror, guilt, nostalgia" (56).

According to Silverman's account of Freud, through repetition and mastery the male "renegotiates his relation to an event by shifting from a passive to an active position" (57). Herr's passive "observer" experience of Vietnam shifts to an active one in writing as he seizes control of the narrative and decides which directions, angles, and forms it will take. This writerly subject position itself serves the function of the denial of castration. Herr twice repeats a compliment offered by grunts that effectively remasculinizes the correspondents: "I got to give it to you, you guys got balls" (206, 207–8). Furthermore, Herr recalls that this verbal rescue once comes from a soldier called Avenger, who "looked like a freshman in divinity school—clear blue eyes, smooth snub nose, cornsilk hair and a look of such trust and innocence that you hoped there would always be someone around to take care of him" (201). Avenger's *whiteness* further reinscribes the racial hierarchies in Herr's relation to black soldiers, for while Avenger may need to be cared for (within the lexicon of the text, presumably by a black grunt), Avenger's *race* confers his ability to reinstate Herr's masculinity. Thus, through the fair-haired one Herr avenges both his masculinity and his writerly subject position by indicating that he would have the grunts' blessing, the assent of the male collective, to compile his narration.

Moreover, the Avenger's symbolic reinstatement of Herr's anatomical masculinity also serves to rescue Herr from intimations of homosexuality. Such intimations pervade Herr's text; they are indicated not only by Herr's defensive need to justify his masculinity and writerly role but also by his ironically self-incriminating reference to press corps members as "closet queens" (228). If, as Antony Easthope claims, "masculinity is defined mainly in the way an individual deals with his femininity and his desire for other men," and "men are really more concerned about other men than about women at all," then *Dispatches* serves as an excellent example of Easthope's definition of sublimation, which "is fundamental to the social order, transforming unacceptable sexual drive into something more conventional" (6). Easthope asserts that in the social order "desexualized, sublimated love for other men becomes available to form the male bond, enabling men to work together for each other" (15). In Herr's text the military becomes a sort of microcosm of the social order in that men work together, much as in Jeffords's formulation of the male collective, for the greater good.

For Jeffords the male collective automatically involves the possibility of homoerotic desire, because membership in the collective is predicated simultaneously upon denial of difference (race, class, education) and affirmation of it (men are *not* like women) (59–60). Because for Jeffords "gender is seen within the vocabulary of the masculine bond as a sexually defined category, the efforts to reaffirm male sexual identity are unavoidable repercussions of its definition" (68). Jeffords believes this affirmation of male sexual identity can only be accomplished through the assertion of heterosexuality, the sexual activity that confirms the male bond. In light of Jeffords's formulation, and Easthope's definition of "present" masculinity, Herr's insistence on his membership in the collective, and therefore his ability to "tell it" (207), also resonates as justificatory when Herr asserts his heterosexuality. He relates how he "shared a great many things" with the grunts, including "field gear, grass, whiskey, girls" (226). And he explains this communal exploitation of women by saying, "That Men Without Women trip got old all the time" (226).

However, one could read this sharing of women as yet another sublimation of homosexual desire—men sublimate aberrant desire, project it onto a female being, then enact the sublimated desire in a manner that validates the social order. In other words, the men effectively displace their desire for one another onto a single woman and hence come as close to homosexuality as the social order will allow.[4] While Herr claims to have participated in such unions, he never describes a particular incident in *Dispatches*.

Rather than positing the communal use of women (i.e., the exchange of women between men) as an example of homosocial heterosexuality, however, I would like to suggest that Herr's parenthetical declaration about the tiresome "trip" endows the erotic exchanges in the text that *do not* involve a woman with greater homosexual intimations.[5] Such exchanges abound within the text. At times Herr merely witnesses them. For example, Herr recalls the moment when a soldier whom he remembers as Swinging Dick reaches down to help his comrade Pray for War to his feet: "Swinging Dick reached down and grabbed his wrists, locking them and pulling him up slowly until their faces were a couple of inches apart. For a second it looked like they were going to kiss" (28). Because the two had just been engaged in a heated exchange of wits, it may just as well have looked as if they were about to spit on one another. Herr, however, foresees a kiss, and the man involved in giving it is Swinging Dick, his name speaking volumes, much like Avenger's, through its placement in this particular recollection. Moreover, Pray for War validates the erotic charge Herr experiences from the near kiss when Pray for War taunts Swinging Dick, whom he calls Scudo: "Mmmm, Scudo, you are really lookin' good, man" (28). No woman exists as intermediary in this exchange. The eroticism Herr witnesses and recollects is male-male.

More often, however, such intimations of homoerotic desire involve Herr as participant instead of spectator. When Herr declares that he and the grunts "were intimate" because "they were my guns, and I let them do it" (67), the statement teems with sexual energy. Even though he means here that the soldiers provided gunfire cover for him, sexual energy issues from an earlier parallel Herr draws between the penis and guns when he characterizes the soldiers' streaming shots as "pee" (62). Beyond this sexualization of technology and violence, and the comparisons of weaponry and male anatomy, on several occasions Herr eroticizes his male acquaintances. Herr seems to carry on infatuations with journalists Sean Flynn, Dana Stone, and Tim Page, and he must have been completely enamored of Avenger to render him descriptively as he does.

But Herr reserves his most admiring attention and lengthiest narrative space for Mayhew, the boyish soldier who, in the words of his comrade Day Tripper, "sleep[s] bare-ass" (129). Herr, indeed, finds Mayhew's nakedness worthy of more than one mention. Mayhew also plays a role in the story of a soldier who jerks off thirty times a day, and he has one of the few expressions of desire by a soldier in the book when he declares that he's "so horny" (137). It comes as no surprise, then, that Herr remembers Mayhew as one grunt who, though not black, "took care" of him (137). Herr recalls waking to incoming fire and seeing Mayhew crouched above him: "He was leaning over me, completely dressed again, his face almost touching mine, and for a second I had the idea that he might have run over to cover me from any possible incoming. (It would not have been the first time that a grunt had done that)" (140). The passage bristles with homoerotic desire. The pose in which Herr awakes to find Mayhew recalls Swinging Dick's near kiss, right down to the statement of time "for a second." Additionally, Herr's semantic construction points to an action not explicitly stated in the passage. If Herr thought at first that Mayhew was there to cover him, what replaced that thought? What was Mayhew indeed there for? The fact that Herr follows the description of Mayhew's posture with a parenthetical statement of the ostensibly normal nature of Mayhew's actions seems to both justify the soldier's behavior and dismiss the desire evident between Herr and Mayhew. Perhaps Herr wished Mayhew was indeed there to cover him, because that action would indicate Mayhew's reciprocal desire for Herr.

I do not present this analysis to prove that Herr is homosexual and that his narrative acts to sublimate his desire. Rather, I wish to suggest, along the lines of theorists Silverman, Jeffords, and Easthope, that homoerotic desire finds little locutive space within the male collective or the Dominant Fiction. Instead, it lurks, unspoken and sublimated, to ensure maintenance of a time-honored ideology about the incompatibility of homosexuality and masculinity. The breach of silence surrounding homosexuality confers a wound upon the playing out of ideology, poignantly illustrated in *Dispatches* when Herr describes a fellow reporter who "heard two Marines lying near him making love" as "looking totally mind blown" (257). Herr describes how the threat of homosexuality registers on his colleague's face as one would depict the physical results of war weaponry. Through his facial expression Herr's associate communicates the Dominant Fiction's tenet that homosexuality, read as rupture of the male body (which in turn challenges unit cohesion and the military order dependent upon intact male bodies), cannot occur within the male collective. In addition, his expression demonstrates societal reluctance to view fictions as fictions, for homoeroticism and homosexuality do, in fact, exist in the armed forces, and war proceeds nonetheless with all its cultural ramifications intact. In this way, then, Herr's text presents messages about the war experience to the civilian public that seem consistently at odds with the manner in which civilian America apprehends war and defines masculinity in relation to it.

## Rupturing the Body: Homosexuality, Race, and the Anticipatory Injury

David Rabe's play *Streamers* attempts to prevent civilian fictions about war as a masculine-verifying enterprise from being read as anything but fictions. The play grants homosexuality the status of a given within the male collective, and black and white soldiers initially appear equal. Homosexuality and race thus emerge as mere differences to be subsumed for the purposes of unit cohesion and survival. But by taking place before the soldiers' deployment, and hence in anticipation of war, the play pushes a wedge between notions of anticipated and actual injuries as Elaine Scarry defines them. Scarry, as noted earlier, claims that "the anticipatory injury is an actual injury" (79). In the setting of Rabe's play, then, the anticipation of injury or death supersedes actual injury, and the characters' fears of bodily impairment resemble Herr's. The characters' attempts to avoid injury combine to deny civilian expectations of soldierly masculinity and thus debunk the time-honored link between participation in a war and the achievement of manhood.

The four principle soldiers in *Streamers,* Roger, Billy, Richie, and Carlyle, occupy identities as diverse as any cross-section of the Vietnam War–era military and thus model the stock units of war narratives in general. Besides Martin, who exits the drama shortly after his suicide attempt, two career military servicemen, sergeants Cokes and Rooney, round out the cast. The veteran soldiers represent America's history of victorious military achievements, but their near-constant state of drunkenness and seeming ineptitude demonstrate how heroic notions from previous American war eras no longer obtain in Vietnam.

The young soldiers, on the other hand, represent the future of the U.S. Armed Forces, especially in terms of integration. Roger is an intelligent and highly motivated African American man. Determined to follow military rules precisely in hopes of bettering his position, Roger keeps the room where he, Richie, and Billy live clean and the floor polished. Additionally, he and Billy regularly execute push-ups to improve their strength. As Roger's comrade in fitness, Billy represents the Dominant Fiction more completely than any of the other characters. Rabe describes Billy as "a white in his mid-twenties, blond and trim" (7), and in his first entrance Billy carries a piece of (apple?) pie he has brought to offer Richie. By alluding to generosity with the character most fully representative of America during the Vietnam era, Rabe introduces an aspect of the Dominant Fiction of the time: the protectorate role that America defended and reproduced by continued engagement in the conflict, in repudiation of Communism. Billy's act of generosity directed toward Richie indicates Billy's care for his comrade, his interest in and contribution to the goal of survival for the male collective. The act also positions Richie as in need of assistance. This position of need—of lack, as it were—dictates that Richie figure as the homosexual in Rabe's play.

The final young soldier in *Streamers* is Carlyle, the second African American man, who initially appears in "filthy fatigues" that are "grease-stained and dark with sweat" (6). While Carlyle's appearance serves primarily to foreshadow his "unclean" actions later in the play, the fact that Carlyle is not entirely put together, in mind or body, also generates various racial stereotypes. The first stereotype emerges when one juxtaposes Carlyle and Roger. Roger clearly represents the "prideful," self-respecting, assimilationist black man, a successful inculcation of military values and hence an ideal postintegration image. Because Carlyle emerges as antithesis to this image, he threatens not only black masculinity, both his and Roger's, but also "unit cohesion." Carlyle's unkemptness, then, accentuates his difference from the other three. Carlyle stands in direct opposition to Billy's representation of the Dominant Fiction because of the myriad ways he represents challenges to the system—race, unbalance, lack of bodily integrity, status as orphan, and status as novice to the others. Ironically, Carlyle also consistently demonstrates the most "successful" use of violent, masculine aggression by appearing to make others behave simply through his force of will.[6]

Rabe's play charts the nascence of the male collective, the elimination of difference, as the boys work together to create their living space—Billy puts down the wax, and Roger spreads it. In addition, at Richie's prompt, Billy attempts to adapt his language patterns to those of the less educated soldiers. Billy says, haltingly, "You ain't . . . shit . . . motherfucker," in order to conceal "just how far beyond the fourth grade [he] went" (12). Like Billy, Carlyle also attempts language alteration in order to move beyond his status as outsider and join the collective. When Carlyle engages in conversation with Roger, a fellow African American, about how Vietnam "ain't our war," he employs a series of "ain'ts" and dropped final *g*'s until Richie enters the room, when he introduces himself, saying, "My name is Carlyle, what is yours?" (19), in what many believe to be standard white English. That Rabe posits this particular English variant as the "norm" that all the soldiers accept for use in the collective perhaps reveals his or the soldiers' hierarchical or prejudicial attitudes about language variation. Or perhaps Rabe wishes to play upon and thus reveal such attitudes in his audience. Nevertheless, both soldiers actually deny a part of their individual identity, expressed in language, in order to achieve and maintain a collective one.[7] This disclaimer of individual identity serves to demonstrate the denial of difference Jeffords deems necessary for the formation of the male collective. Carlyle appears to have fully infiltrated the system not only because the boys allow him to spend the night in their room but also because they engage in social activities outside the barracks with him. Carlyle's position inside the collective enables him to lodge a greater threat to its function through the intimations of his homosexuality and also serves to highlight the mythic nature of societal belief in the absence of homoerotic desire in the male collective or the military.

Homosexuality exists in David Rabe's play not as a predetermined and static, self-claimed identity, but in the many fissures in masculine desire and actions that belie the signification of true heterosexuality. These ruptures lodge in the consciousness of society at large in the form of stereotypes, and the play appears to unveil the fictional nature of these stereotypes by suggesting the possibility of truth in them. For instance, society often uses the statement "the critic doth protest too much" to identify closeted homosexuals expressing disgust for homosexuality. Several manifestations of such defensive male posturing allude to possible homosexuality in the play. In one example Roger tells Carlyle that the poster of the naked woman in Richie's locker evidences that "this here the locker of a faggot" (16). While Roger reads Richie's placement of the poster as a defense against accusations of homosexuality, what does it mean that, of all the boys, Roger is the one seen most often viewing *Playboy*? A second intimation of homosexuality concerns Richie's conflation of sex and exercise when Billy and Roger do push-ups. Richie insists on the erotic element of the activity, and Roger defensively responds, "We was exercisin' Richie. You heard a that?" (46). Roger's retort indicates an attempt to exonerate his actions, which he seeks through a critique not only of Richie's body but also of Richie's knowledge. Finally, when Roger invites Billy to join him and Carlyle at the whorehouse, Richie claims that Billy would be "scared to death in a cathouse," to which Billy protests emphatically, "BULLSHIT!" (56).

Homosexuality also emerges in the classic arena of reduced inhibitions, illustrated through the drunken sergeants Cokes and Rooney. As Antony Easthope suggests, "alcohol makes permissible a personal intimacy otherwise frowned upon" (65). When the two sergeants enter the boys' quarters and Rooney announces Cokes's recent return from Vietnam, the two nearly kiss when Rooney hugs Cokes. The intimacy of their bodily proximity reads innocuously because of alcohol-reduced inhibitions, and reduced inhibitions simultaneously present the actions as they might "truly" be if not repressed. In another scene involving alcohol Richie takes advantage of Carlyle's drunken stupor to cover him with a blanket and pat his arm. This stage direction suggests that a man under the influence may be more responsive to a homosexual advance. When interrogated in sum, the intimations of homosexual desire in the play indicate that once the specter of homosexuality has been raised, every action signifies more intensely because of the necessary disavowal of homoerotic desire.[8]

However, homosexuality in Rabe's play remains unconstituted in actions that typically describe it. Carlyle desires that Richie suck his "big black boy," his "thing," his "rope" (48), and one night upon his return from a binge, Carlyle opportunistically demands that Richie do so. In addition, Carlyle continually refers to the men around him as "cute," but he is never read as queer by his fellow soldiers, who heap the blame for the sexual tension in the room upon the self-avowed homosexual, Richie. Carlyle provides the soldiers with transportation to a whorehouse and enables their heterosexuality while affirming his own: "They send me over to that Vietnam, I be cool, 'cause I been dodgin' bullets and shit since I been old enough to get on pussy make it happy to know me. I can get on, I can do my job" (51). Carlyle's final "I can get on" makes a connection between heterosexual function—"get on pussy make it happy to know me"—and soldierly survival, as if the latter depended upon the former.

This is not the first instance in the play where battle ability depends upon heterosexual function. When the subject of homosexuality first enters *Streamers,* in a discussion between Roger and Billy, the boys not only attempt to discern the truth about Richie's sexual preference—"you don't really think he means that shit he talks, do you?" (14)—but also imagine what it would be like to be in battle with him. Billy's comment, "Can you imagine bein' in combat with Richie—people blasting away at you—he'd probably want to hold your hand" (13), indicates that Richie's alleged homosexuality renders him incapable of military service. The play never challenges the *legality* of Richie's service, given prohibitions on gay servicemembers during Vietnam, and hence effectively signals the acknowledged presence of homosexuality in the military.

However, in another assay to form the masculine bond and the male collective, the boys, despite their suspicions that Richie indeed does mean what he says, attempt to accommodate the possibility of his homosexuality. Reversing his earlier assessment, Roger claims that the *Playboy* photo in Richie's locker evidences Richie's heterosexuality, and Billy responds that even if Richie were gay, "some of 'em are okay guys" (14). Obviously, Billy's defense of Richie is formed out of his own relationship to his childhood friend Frankie, after whom Rabe originally titled the play. Billy's defense, however tenuously modeled on a character outside of the play, introduces the possibility of "unit cohesion" despite homosexuality. The collective attempt to accept Richie's sexuality appears to succeed until Richie and Carlyle's nearly consummated sex act, because Billy wants to leave the light on and Roger insists on remaining within the room while the sex occurs. While Roger and Billy putatively accede to gay sex in their presence out of an insistence that they not be forced to leave, the scene can also be interpreted as another example of how the masculine collective elides difference. Quite possibly, the boys had sex in one another's presence while at the whorehouse. Homosexuality almost becomes like heterosexuality in this scene—the acts are tolerated, even if not engaged in, by all members of the collective.

However, the intimation of sex between Richie and Carlyle eventually leads to the scuffle in which Carlyle kills Billy, and the murder indicates that homosexuality can be countenanced within an anticipatory realm but not within the real, within the locutive but not within the performative/perforative. As the agent of the brutalities, Carlyle signifies on a number of levels. First, because he is not only African American but originally figures outside the collective, all the threats he poses to that collective emerge as destructive of it. Second, his race also signifies the failure of integration to create "unit cohesion," for though the specter of homosexuality precipitates the disaster, race brings it to fruition—Carlyle is black, but not read as gay.

Race figures as well immediately after Billy's death, as Roger and Richie proceed to clean up Billy's blood. Roger becomes so enraged with Richie's insistence that Billy did want to "hold his hand" (78) that he "slams the bucket into the corner and rams the mop into the bucket. Furious, he marches down to Richie" (78, stage direction), only to be interrupted by Cokes entering the room. Because of the *anticipation* of injury contained in the action, Roger's move with intent to harm Richie indicates the dissolution of the male collective, the reinstatement of notions of difference. But Billy's *actual* injury by Carlyle, which, like the averted Roger/Richie conflict, occurs across lines of race, represents the collapse of the Dominant Fiction and its attendant beliefs through the rupture inflicted upon Billy's bodily envelope. When the play's representative of the Dominant Fiction dies, the young men realize that homosexuality *does* exist. An anticipatory injury no longer equals a real injury, as Scarry claims, for only through an *actual* wound have the soldiers been able to understand the threat of homosexuality and the dubiousness of their beliefs. When Roger insists that Richie "shoulda jus' tole ole Roger" (77), the fact that Richie *had* told him renders telling insufficient and demonstrates that only experience can establish fact, that only the body can reveal truth. In order to do so, the body must remain inviolate, and the play suggests the impossibility of its doing so.

Although refuting her equation of anticipatory and actual injuries by lodging truth in the body, *Streamers* supports Scarry's discussion of injury as the "object of war," in which the visibility of wounds on the body memorializes war (114). John C. Dibble notices society's demand for the "object of war" when he says that "for many people, the war so defied understanding that they needed some physical manifestation—a wound—to help them comprehend it" (28). Furthermore, homosexuality produces ruptures in all of the components of "immaterial culture," which Scarry lists as "national consciousness, political belief and self-definition" (114). The fear of these ruptures emerges poignantly in the military policy on the incompatibility of homosexuality and service. The military, as guarantor of "national consciousness and political belief," the protector of the right to "self-definition" (for heterosexuals, at least), cannot countenance rupture, as revealed by the "mind-blown" soldier in Herr's memoirs and the collapse of the masculine collective at the end of Rabe's play.

Scarry also argues for persistence in "the relation between body and belief" (115), the coherence of the former enabling the endurance of the latter, the possibility of which both works dismiss. Unlike the Dominant Fiction, Scarry's notion of belief does not entail belief in a fiction, but rather belief in an absolute truth lodged in the body. For the young soldiers in Rabe's play, the rupture of Billy's body results in belief in homosexuality, in injury, and in death; the concepts become real for them only *after* the injury, and masculinity is no buttress against them. Herr, on the other hand, notes the incongruity between bodily coherence and belief when he speaks of what it means to be a "survivor" for correspondents: "The more you moved the more you saw, the more you saw the more besides death and mutilation you risked" (8). Correspondents, Herr says, "came to fear something more complicated than death, an annihilation less final but more complete" (243). By Herr's own admission this fear emasculates him and remains long after his return to "The World." For the soldiers in *Streamers* injury creates belief; for Herr injury to belief systems results even though he returns with his bodily envelope intact. Both *Streamers* and *Dispatches* demonstrate, then, what Yossarian learns opening Snowden's flak jacket: when bodies are called upon to guarantee belief in fictions, something is bound to disintegrate and slither away.

# WINNING
# THIS TIME

*The War That Wasn't*

### Synchronizing War Narratives

**The war against Iraq did not bring stability to the Middle East, did not establish U.S. hegemony in the region or geopolitically around the globe, did not prevent necessary military budget cuts, did not guarantee the reelection of George Bush, and, crucially, did not get rid of Saddam Hussein.**
—Douglas Kellner, "From Vietnam to the Gulf: Postmodern Wars?"

In *The Great War and Modern Memory* Paul Fussell connects the process of "training in military maneuver and technique" with the structure of the "paradigm" war memoir. Fussell claims that both follow a three-step development: "first, preparation; then execution; and finally, critique" (130). The narrative elements shared by the training procedure and the chronological reconstruction of war experience—their respective beginnings, middles, and ends—allow Fussell to make his comparison in the first place. Likewise, in *The Body in Pain* Elaine Scarry describes "the essential structure of war" as comprised of narrative elements. This "structure," she writes, "resides in the relation between its own largest parts, the relation between the collective casualties that occur within war, and the verbal issues . . . that stand outside war, that are there before the act of war begins and after it ends, that are understood by warring populations as the motive and justification and will again be recognized after the war as the thing substantiated or (if one is on the losing side) not substantiated by war's activity" (63). Thus, Scarry includes both the buildup to and the recovery from war in war's structure. Marilyn Wesley summarizes the implications of Scarry's theory for war writing in a way that extends and impacts Fussell's search for a paradigm of combatants' memoirs. Wesley writes, in *Violent Adventure,* that "war stories are not secondary reflections about war but part of its essential operation" (91). In other words, the stories nations tell themselves about war eras are necessary to fully understand how war happens and what it means.

The divergent historical narratives the title of this chapter encompasses are, if not known explicitly, certainly familiar to many present-day Americans, and that familiarity attests to the processes of historicizing war that Fussell, Scarry, and Wesley describe. Specifically, the title, "Winning This Time," alludes to two narratives presently at work historicizing the First Gulf War (1991) in civilian American culture. The first is Jean Baudrillard's repeated and unfortunate characterization of the war's hyperreality, its existence as what he calls a "fourth phase simulation" (1933), and the second is George Pan Cosmatos's 1985 film *Rambo: First Blood II,* starring Sylvester Stallone. When inquiring about his mission to return to Vietnam to rescue prisoners of war, Stallone's John Rambo famously asks, "Do we get to win it this time?"

Lynda Boose claims that Rambo's line "helped to produce the angst it reflected over the issue that by 1985 had come to traumatize the national psyche"—that the "withdrawal" from Vietnam had created a sense of "abandoned" masculinity and "shame" (590). This sense, Boose continues, "[lay] behind the revalorized aggressiveness of the national character" (587), which "retrenched" masculine values and "reformulated" the Vietnam problem as "the failure to deploy [militarized] values strongly enough" (586).[1] Rambo's return to refight thus reflects America's cultural necessity to revise, indeed rewrite, not only its *critique* but also its *execution* of Vietnam, a necessity so pervasive it was used to enable and justify the Persian Gulf War of 1991.

Calling preparation for the 1991 war "the rebirth of American militarism," Douglas Kellner argues that "the Vietnam generation military who suffered defeat in Vietnam," among whom he identifies "Norman Schwarzkopf, Colin Powell, and other generals and midlevel career military," yearned to "win big this time, to overcome the Vietnam syndrome, to redeem the U.S. military, to recover their manhood and self-esteem—and perhaps protect the Pentagon budget from overzealous cuts" (216). In positing "winning big this time" as the endpoint of the First Gulf War, what Fussell would call its "critique," the U.S. military not only refought and won Vietnam (and hence revived flagging American masculinity) but also wrote the history of Operation Desert Storm before Desert Shield had even been activated.

Or did they?

In this chapter I argue that the American desire to synchronize the rewritten execution of the Vietnam War (and, by extension, the war's outcome) with victory in Operation Desert Storm creates uncanny flashbacks to the "essential structure" of the Vietnam War in critical appraisals and cultural representations of the First Gulf War. The chapter contends that the predetermined "end" of the First Persian Gulf War, meant to give shape to both itself and its predecessor, has instead robbed the cultural imaginary of the "critique" Fussell and Scarry locate as central to the processing of war and hamstrung the imaginary at Fussell's "execution" stage. In other words, unable to fully process "what happened" in Vietnam, America has attempted to rescript the military defeat via the anticipated victory of the First Gulf War.

My readings of David O. Russell's *Three Kings* and Anthony Swofford's *Jarhead* demonstrate that we are still fighting the Vietnam War yet still unable to accept Desert Storm's victory as such. This chapter identifies theoretical debates over the nature of the war and cultural representations of it as indicative of an American inability to reconcile the First Gulf War with previous concepts of victory or to see it as rectifying "the Vietnam problem": to view the war as new, much less on its own terms, disables its signifying relationship with the earlier conflict and hence that war's closure; but to conceive of the war as the end of "the Vietnam syndrome" threatens Desert Storm's historical existence and brings us back to Baudrillard's conclusion. Hence, this chapter's subtitle is intended not to flippantly elide the very real experiences of Iraqi civilians, combat participants, and families on both sides during the 1991 engagement, but to suggest the narrative costs, in the American cultural imagination, of positing historical ends as their beginnings. Thus presented, *Three Kings* and *Jarhead* register serious counterassaults on the civilian understanding of war; by narrating soldiers' experience of war, both these texts highlight the persistent gap *Male Armor* delineates.

As in previous war eras, late twentieth-century definitions of American masculinity emerge as implicated in and indicative of the United States' sense of self during and after the First Persian Gulf War, so symptoms of cultural difficulties in narrativizing Operation Desert Storm imbue representations of the war. This chapter examines Russell's 1999 film and Swofford's 2003 memoir not only as barometers of contemporaneous depictions of masculinity but also as reflections of American society's assays in accommodating a war whose narrative outcome predated its historical resolution—indeed, its commencement. While *Three Kings* posits versions of masculinity ostensibly influenced by theoretical understandings of gender emergent post-second-wave feminism and after the 1975 Fall of Saigon, it does so by trumpeting American beneficence. Having been deployed to help the culture navigate imputations of American brutality in Vietnam, the narrative of "good cause despite horrendous effect" reiterates the Vietnam War, while also denying the preordained conclusion of Operation Desert Storm.[2] By beginning after "the war has just ended" (*Three Kings*), the movie suggests the nebulous nature of the victory and resorts to Vietnam-era recuperations of the conflict. Since these recuperations have the "syndrome" or "problem" of Vietnam built into their structure, *Three Kings* effectively enervates any subversive images of masculinity it presents and narratively reduces Operation Desert Storm to a retelling of the Vietnam conflict, in other words, to a cipher.

After a brief "present-day" vignette that sets the scene for its writing, Anthony Swofford's *Jarhead* follows Fussell's developmental model for the war memoir, although it is stylistically and topically indebted to Vietnam War narratives, including Michael Herr's *Dispatches* and Tim O'Brien's *If I Die in a Combat Zone* and *The Things They Carried*, to which *Jarhead* is frequently, though unjustifiably, compared. These inheritances disrupt Swofford's ability to offer either a critique of Operation Desert Storm to match its predicted outcome or a pacifying conclusion for the war's predecessor. Though Swofford steers the memoir toward an antiwar stance with the potential to discourage future revisionist warring, Swofford's superficial battle in deconstructing the "masculinity and war feedback loop" and the redolent self-pity permeating the memoir essentially cloud, if not render moot, its cautionary tale for readers. Moreover, in featuring its subject's "spectator" status in the desert, *Jarhead* encourages both the anesthetized image of modern warfare and the historical erasure of the First Gulf War. Despite all protestations to the contrary, then, the jarhead whom Swofford presents at least enables the belief that a more traditionally heroic experience of the war (i.e., a more masculinist one) might have produced a different man in Swofford's recollections.

If *Rambo: First Blood II* posits imagistically the body necessary to "win it this time," and if, as Douglas Kellner contends, "the war against Iraq . . . was formulated as an attempt to avoid 'another Vietnam' and to overcome 'the Vietnam syndrome'" (226), then both America's preferred definitions of masculinity and its sense of national self are highly implicated in Operation Desert Storm. Joshua Goldstein surmises that the "recent manhood type— exemplified by 'Rambo'—centers on autonomy" and that the "ultimate duty he owes is to personal excellence" (282). As the First Gulf War played out, however, little room for "personal excellence" seemed extant for the combatants, so representational accounts of the conflict typically depict images of masculinity inconsistent with the traditional soldier-hero. In the opening vignettes of *Jarhead,* Anthony Swofford recollects the "magic brutality" of the war films that the basic-training recruits rent in an effort to imagine themselves as the soldiers they are about to become. Yet Swofford recounts a soldiering for the moviegoers that is already disconnected from the excellence and honor that narratives posit for it when he admits that "somehow the films convince us that these boys are sweet, even though we know we are much like these boys and that we are no longer sweet" (6–7). In *Three Kings,* when Major Archie Gates (played by George Clooney) tells his superior, "I don't even know what we did here," he adroitly summarizes both the soldier's inability to demonstrate the autonomous excellence of his training and public uncertainty about how to describe or define, indeed how to "win," Operation Desert Storm.

This uncertainty about categorizing the First Gulf War also colors theoretical and critical discussions of the war, which frequently focus either upon the technological and/or mediated components of the conflict or upon individual soldiers' experiences of the war as vehicles for qualifying the war as a whole. For instance, in connecting the use of new technology in the Persian

Gulf to the American government's highly controlled media depiction of the war's events, Douglas Kellner concludes that Operation Desert Storm, not Vietnam, emerges as the first postmodern war. He writes that the First Gulf War "was postmodern in that, first, it was experienced by most of the world . . . as a carefully manufactured attempt to mobilize consent to U.S. policy, in which the distinction between truth and reality seemed to blur, and image and spectacle prevailed. Second, the war itself exhibited a new implosion between individuals and technology. . . . Thirdly, the war was a form of cyberwar, with information technology and new smart weapons systems prominently displayed (albeit excessively hyped). Thus, the Gulf War deployed both a new mode of high-tech warfare and a new experience of war as a hyperreal media event . . . that demonstrated a new way to exploit 'war' and new types of global political manipulation" (218). Much like Jean Baudrillard, Kellner clearly wishes for readers to conceive of the First Gulf War as entirely driven by technological innovation and recorded as computerized imagery.

In a relatively rare overlap of the two poles of theoretical discussions of Operation Desert Storm, Margot Norris, in *Writing War in the Twentieth Century,* employs the postmodern types and uses of technology to argue specifically about their connections to soldiering. She suggests that "dramatic changes in the technology of weaponry in the twentieth century . . . effectively deconstruct the concept of the warrior and of combatancy in ways that make the Hegelian gladiatorial and masculinist model of individual one-on-one combat philosophically obsolete and irrelevant for understanding modern war" (17). In her argument Norris is clear to qualify the impact wrought by technological changes, as implicated in philosophical discussions of war, the type of discussion that Kellner presents as part of cultural negotiation and historicization of war.

But the reduction of war to its theoretical aftereffects sits uncomfortably with some who concentrate on the opposite pole: the soldier. Surely, Norris's need to note that she speaks of *philosophical* discussions of war mirrors Alex Vernon's impulse, in *Soldiers Once and Still,* to distinguish critics' labeling of war. In his persistent focus on "those who fought the war" (14), Vernon resists the "intellectual assertion that any war exhibits formal, aesthetic characteristics with literature, art, and other forms of cultural expression" (17), which he associates with critical connections drawn between Vietnam and postmodernism in literature and the arts. Labeling such connections "myth," Vernon notes that "to say that the cultural dynamic driving economics and the arts also manifested itself on the battlefield is to refute what soldiers have always known: terrain dictates. The jungle, not the culture of late capitalism, made Vietnam into the fragmented, chaotic mess of small unit combat, just as the Arabian desert shaped the Persian Gulf War's maneuver-heavy, long distance battlefield" (12). Vernon's specific connection between Vietnam and the First Gulf War, of which he is a veteran, indicates theoretical disagreement over classifying Operation Desert Storm. But Vernon's assertion that the two are essentially alike also paradoxically suggests both the need to validate the short 1991 engagement and its potential for eclipse by the Vietnam War.

Vernon's resistance to cultural or aesthetic encoding of war parallels and impacts the distinction he feels must be maintained between soldierly experience of war and critical, theoretical, or philosophical discussions of war, which usually come *after* a war's completion, as the theorists presented here all indicate. While this distinction lies at the heart of *Male Armor*'s study, it emerges as especially problematic in the First Gulf War. The public experienced Operation Desert Storm largely through television screens, in a seemingly "live" format that was also highly anesthetized and corpseless.[3] The soldiers, on the other hand, experienced a war that appears, at least in cultural, aesthetic representations, to have barely existed at all, much less to have offered the traditional heroic masculinity promised either in previous wars or in the culture's imagination of war's purpose and effects. Vernon correctly argues that soldiers on the ground continue to do the things they've always done and that their experience hence underwent little change in late twentieth-century wars. Yet, I contend, even soldierly experience of the First Gulf War cannot be separated from representations of it in the culture's imagination, as representation likely influences cultural memory more than historical or theoretical reflection, though all these aspects certainly comprise the war's structure as defined by Elaine Scarry. Many soldiers, though surely not all, also experienced the war as the culture witnessed it—live, televised, or on a computer radar screen—instead of as traditional warriors. Moreover, because public discussion utilized to justify the war partly couched Desert Shield and Desert Storm in terms rectifying the history of the Vietnam conflict, the soldiers expected the engagement in the desert to feel like the Vietnam-era movies and music they had grown up on.[4]

Offering an adroit coalescence of the intersections among Vietnam, the

First Gulf War, American self-definition, and masculinity, Lynda Boose, in her article "Techno-Muscularity and the 'Boy Eternal,'" describes soldierly experience of the First Gulf War specifically through the versions of American masculinity the soldiers were trained to support. These versions, Boose claims, hail from the Vietnam War and the protests against it. Boose analyzes "the official rhetoric connecting America's massive intervention in the Gulf with 'overcoming the Vietnam syndrome'" and declares George H. W. Bush's "domestic policy" emergent in the 1991 invasion of Iraq an attempt "to bury in the desert the antiwar discourse signified by 'Vietnam'" (583). The first President Bush's rhetoric, Boose claims, reduced "remembered opposition to the Vietnam War into competing narratives so that one could be reclaimed from its antiwar affiliations and the other one anathematized." As Boose understands it, the "more global narrative that the Gulf War was target to excise" involved "the morality of America's foreign policy and military conduct and its impact on both the Vietnamese people and American soldiers" (584). The recuperable narrative, on the other hand, was one of "strict containment; the war was restricted to a focus on the individual American soldier." Writing prior to 1993, Boose not only astutely recounts collective historicizing of the Vietnam War but also presciently describes the narrative trajectories of cultural critiques of the First Gulf War, including *Three Kings* and *Jarhead*. Both of these narratives of Operation Desert Storm adopt and adapt cultural rescripting of Vietnam, and an examination of how the texts undertake this endeavor reveals both the limits of America's attempt to rewrite Vietnam with a victorious end and the inevitable purchase on masculinity of its foreordained conclusion. Largely because of the immense signification brought to bear upon Operation Desert Storm—as healing Vietnam, as involving no collateral damage—representations of the conflict emerge as already participating in the culture's narrativizing of the war, as if Fussell's three steps and Scarry's structure have coalesced into a single moment predicted before it materialized. The impossibility of such a confluence reveals itself in these productions as confused disillusion, but, more importantly for American national identity and sense of self, as antiheroic or unmanly, as these terms are traditionally defined.[5] Though the texts reimagine cultural narratives meant to assuage the Vietnam syndrome, as Boose defines them, neither *Three Kings* nor *Jarhead* has yet convinced the American public of the efficacy of their revised soldier-heroes.

## "Holding Out for a Hero": AWOL Revisited

He's gotta be sure and he's gotta be soon
And he's gotta be larger than life
—Jim Steinman and Dean Pitchford, "Holding Out for a Hero" (1984)

David O. Russell's *Three Kings* will likely keep viewers holding out, because it denies the image of the traditional hero imagined in Steinman and Pitchford's lyrics. The 1999 film exhibits both foci Lynda Boose delineates for representations of Vietnam, the one "on the individual soldier" and the one "on the morality of America's foreign policy and military conduct" (584). This reversion to prior modes of narrating war, indeed to prior wars, seems both contradictory to Operation Desert Storm—given theoretical focus upon technological newness; a new war ought to demand new modes of telling—and fully aligned with its cultural inscription as finally winning for its predecessor. I would suggest, however, that as a narrative representation of the First Gulf War, *Three Kings* indicates that cultural memory has merely reproduced the historical realities of the United States' involvement in Vietnam and marked them with the trappings of this ostensibly new type of war. In other words, *Three Kings* rewrites the historical chapter on Vietnam but fails to close it. What do emerge as changed, however, are the images of masculinity the film presents, but since these cannot be contained within the traditional modes of heroic soldiering victory demands, the heroes of the film ostensibly cannot be heroes at all; they must go AWOL, and they must be kings. As the movie's tagline indicates, "In a war without heroes they are kings."

The nature of this monarchy emerges during the film's opening sequence. Set after the ceasefire has been issued in "March 1991," when "the war has just ended," the scene depicts a small unit of soldiers traversing a bleak landscape much like a dried-up seabed. They are temporarily halted, having come upon an unsurrendered Iraqi soldier standing, armed, upon a small rise in the desert. Mark Wahlberg, whose character has yet to be introduced to viewers, loudly asks his comrades whether or not, given the end of the war, they're "shooting." When no definitive response is forthcoming from his otherwise-engaged peers, Wahlberg proceeds to shoot his adversary, and the camera zooms with the bullet toward the target, whom it reveals to be pulling a white flag from the pocket of his military uniform. Viewers will later learn, when the film cuts to an actual surrender-directive card dropped upon the fleeing Iraqi Army by U.S. helicopters, that the soldier's surrender was not according to protocol, but this does not justify his shooting. Spike Jonze's character exclaims, "Damn, I didn't think I'd get to see anybody shot in this war."

This opening sequence cogently illustrates the discordant narratives of masculinity, resonant for contemporaneous viewers, that have come to influence both the war's historicization and the public's ability to negotiate it: prohibited by the technological thrust and chronological brevity of Operation Desert Storm from shooting the enemy, and hence from defining themselves as men, the soldiers must resort to amoral transgression of the ceasefire, to nonheroic action, in order to realize the manhood they'd gone to war to achieve in the first place. By portraying such unmanly, indeed un-American, actions as the introduction for the film, Russell begins to deconstruct the American certainty of heroic masculinity. But because this is a war film about Americans featuring hugely popular Hollywood stars, he also necessitates the film's rescue of his kings, as nothing but a "good" narrative suffices for the Hollywood action film.

As the opening credits roll, Russell treats viewers to the scene of a desert party purportedly celebrating American "victory." The sequence models desert imagery made familiar via constant broadcasting of Desert Shield and Desert Storm, right down to its absence of conflict, which civilians experienced only as computerized blips, green tracers on a black screen. Besides drinking illegally in host-country Saudi Arabia, the soldiers, both men and women, are shown dancing to music, lifting weights, and sunbathing.[6] The notable exception to the revelry is George Clooney's character, introduced as Major Archie Gates, "two weeks from retirement," who expresses concern to his commanding officer over "what we did here." Countervailing the imagery of the party, Russell depicts Gates in the midst of a slow-motion sandstorm kicked up when a helicopter lifts off. This brief, blurred sequence constitutes the viewers' only moment for pause, as at another point in the opening Russell films Gates from behind, seated before a wall of computers and television screens, with a female reporter astride him. This rather blatant reference to the military "fucking the media" deflates through humor any critique of the media's role in narrating and historicizing that the film may hope to register through Gates's question and his sandstorm pause.

While not removing Archie Gates from heterosexual function, and thus from manhood altogether, Gates's sex scene certainly diminishes his heroic possibilities by positing his libidinal pursuits as recompense for his sense of dissatisfaction with his war experience.

In fact, viewers quickly learn that the film's veterans all pursue personal pleasure and/or gain as a means to staunch their disillusionment with the war and their own role in it. During the next day's official activities, the soldiers are shown surrendering Iraqi Army soldiers, this time in the appropriate manner, as displayed on the cards: disrobing them and searching their bodies for weapons and intelligence. In one such search army reservists Troy Barlow (Mark Wahlberg) and Conrad Vig (Spike Jonze) discover a rolled-up map concealed not so expertly in the rectum of a surrendering Iraqi. Having missed out on a sense of adventure in the war, and having heard rumors of luxury items looted from Kuwait by Saddam Hussein's army, the soldiers immediately suspect that the map reveals the proverbial pot at the end of the rainbow, the millions in Kuwaiti bullion plundered by Hussein's army.

This find commences the action sequence of the film, as Barlow and Vig quickly enlist Chief Elgin (Ice Cube) and foment a plan for liberating the stash for their pecuniary benefit, some souvenirs, and a sense of satisfaction. As word of the map's discovery spreads throughout base camp, Archie Gates discerns the potential not only to experience previously lacking fulfillment but to create a story for his media charge, NBS reporter and five-time Emmy runner-up Adriana Cruz (Nora Dunn). Gates commandeers the map; establishes control over the reservists, whom he quickly demonstrates to be inferior in training or intellect by revealing the "real" map to Saddam's bunkers that the "Iraqi ass map" conceals; and hatches a secret plan for looting the bunkers. Vig, Barlow, Elgin, and Walter Wogaman (Jamie Kennedy) immediately pledge their allegiance and secrecy when Gates promises that the bunkers indeed contain the Kuwaiti bullion. Claiming that he has "no problem stealing the gold from Saddam" for their benefit, Gates presents an image of a less-than-honorable soldier, an image, Peter Jones argues, that "[reflects] accurately a mood of the times," when "the desire to serve one's nation, the lust for reputation or place, the aura of intrinsic merit that has traditionally been attached to military service" have all been "enormously vitiated" (164). Ironically, the "recent books about war" Jones discusses cover the Vietnam conflict, as his study was published in 1976, but his description accurately captures the mood Russell conveys for soldiers participating in the First Gulf War. *Three Kings* thus here models attitudes and imagery consistent with, rather than opposed to or rectifying, Vietnam War representations.

This is not to say that *Three Kings* merely reproduces Vietnam War movies in a different locale with a different landscape. At the very least the picture reflects images the public had already come to associate with the First Gulf War because of the nearly incessant media coverage of Desert Shield and Desert Storm. It was these images, rather than those of previous war films, that Russell aimed to replicate. Filmed on location between Phoenix and Tucson, the movie recaptures what Russell, however reductively, describes as the complete "bleakness" of the Iraqi landscape. Russell carefully presents resonant images of both the buildup to and the execution of the war, including the mind-numbing waiting in the desert that the soldiers filled by lifting weights, sunbathing, giving one another haircuts, listening to music, even arguing about the makes and models of cars. Likewise, *Three Kings* references combat details familiar to many Americans, including the soldiers' "mission oriented protective posture" (MOPP) suits, meant to shield them against chemical weapons; the night-vision goggles that Walter tries to use during the day (ostensibly because he had no nighttime missions); and the threat posed by pervasive landmines. Additionally, in his attempt to provide "new information" to "self-satisfied Americans" about this "un-examined," "morally compromised" war (as he states on the DVD's "Director's Commentary"), Russell and scriptwriter John Ridley fashion plotlines about the ever-present camera and film crews and the military escorts they required. One commanding officer tells Archie Gates that "this is a media war, so you better get on board," thus expressing the U.S. military's concern with appropriate appearance, rather than honorable intention. Moreover, *Three Kings* chillingly depicts the environmental devastation resulting from the war's execution, including petroleum-sodden Ukrainian pelicans coated by the pollution from burning oil wells. Cruz's subplot also displays the American eagerness to forget such atrocities: the reporter asserts that the pollution story "has been so done" already and manages to summon only clearly forced and insincere regret over the damaged birds.

Perhaps the most resolutely new element of *Three Kings* lies in the innovative film-making techniques Russell employs: the types of lenses and filters utilized, the varied foci they allow, and the editing and film coloration processes undertaken in the studio. Russell explains many of these practices in the DVD's "Director's Commentary," including techniques to re-create the immense light created by sunlight reflecting off of sand; filters that produce a grainy, live-video appearance; and lenses that allow for simultaneous close-up and long focus, as when the soldiers discover the "ass map." Another innovation also appears to provide the reexamination of the war that Russell intends: the repetitive display of the results of war injury on an ostensibly real body.[7] In one such scene, as Gates describes sepsis effects to his reservist charges, the film depicts the entry of a bullet into a body, its trajectory inside the body cavity, and its rupture of the gall bladder, replete with a brilliant green seepage of bile. In another, after Barlow has been shot, Gates explains how to treat a sucking chest wound, created when a bullet hole allows air to enter the body cavity and crush the lungs, suffocating the victim. In order to remedy this crushing effect, Gates pokes a thick needle, outfitted with a valve, into Barlow's lung. Gates demonstrates how the valve can be opened to reinflate the lung, and the film cuts back and forth between Gates's demonstration and an internal view of the effects of the treatment in the body. Russell's highly medicalized and repetitious use of the body introduces viewers to something anesthetized, real-time, "hyperreal" representations of war never showed—the effects of war on the body—and encourages them to consider that Operation Desert Storm may not have been as corpseless as the military and media would have them believe.

This focus on the bodily injury of an American, however, should not be misconstrued as representing the narrative focus on honor that Lynda Boose classifies as the recuperative narrative of representation of the Vietnam conflict, because the film depicts the wound as a consequence of the soldiers' attempted seizure of Iraqi bullion for *their own* benefit. In other words, the entrepreneurial self-focus of the soldiers at the center of *Three Kings* continues to disavow their traditional definitions as soldier-heroes. The first body sequence, a mere example, foreshadows Barlow's actual chest wound, and the anticipated injury becomes real for Barlow when he's shot, and Russell thus accomplishes Elaine Scarry's claim, in *The Body in Pain*, that "the anticipatory injury is an actual injury" (79). The wound also does not beg audience pity because it figures as an expected stumbling block in the resolution of the plot to steal Kuwaiti gold from Saddam, the narrative thrust of the film. Russell claims that the traditional Hollywood action plot diverges from the typically character-driven vehicles of his film-making career to this point and in fact insists that the film downplays the roles of individual characters.[8] If, however, Russell intends for the film to radically alter American perceptions of the war and to make "confident, self-satisfied Americans" (as Russell says) uncomfortable with their moral rectitude, something must give, because the film seems largely crafted to portray these "kings" as a metaphorical representation of American exploitation of the conflict, a representation that, at least initially, appears only to substitute real gold for "black gold."

*Three Kings* attempts to rescue both its narrative trajectory and the monarchical status of its lead characters when, in the process of absconding with millions in gold bullion, the film's four opportunists witness the brutal slaying of a rebel Iraqi mother by remnants of Saddam's army who guard the bunker in the village where the gold is stored. Told by the Iraqi Army that they cannot intervene, under the protocol established during the ceasefire, which they have nevertheless already violated, the U.S. soldiers are eventually drawn into the local disagreement when one of the Iraqi soldiers fires upon the plundering Americans. The Americans recognize their responsibility to assist the democratic uprising of the Iraqi rebels, whose insurrection the George H. W. Bush administration had encouraged but ultimately failed to support upon liberation of wealthy, but undemocratic, Kuwait from Saddam Hussein's invading forces. Russell thus places the responsibility for a rescue of Bush administration policies upon his four entrepreneurs and effectively sets them up as traitors—to do their "American" duty by the Iraqi rebels, the opportunists must disobey the American military and wrongheaded military policy and become rebels themselves. Calling Gates's "moral shift" to help the Iraqi rebels a "victory," Lila Kitaeff contends that "by the script focusing on that victory, it [the script] somehow compensates for the failures of the war itself" (8). In one fell swoop, then, the film begins its critique of the American mission and embarks upon rendering heroes.

The remainder of *Three Kings* follows the soldiers as they escape the village with the Kuwaiti bullion and their newfound Iraqi rebel charges but without Barlow, who's been seized by the Iraqi Army forces. Barlow's capture necessitates his rescue, which Gates and the other reservists accomplish by staging Saddam's approach to the village with the help of the rebels, whose vehicles they hire to use for the mock-up. By the time the troupe rescues Barlow, and Barlow receives his chest wound and Conrad Vig dies, the U.S. Army has pieced together Gates's plan. Knowing that they will face certain courts-martial, the soldiers hatch a scheme to successfully remedy the many concurrent disasters their heist has precipitated: they will transfer the Iraqi rebels to Iran, conceal Vig's death, retain some of their plunder, and save their own skins in the face of sedition.

They accomplish their absolution, of course, via the media. They recruit Adriana Cruz, assigned to Archie Gates, to film them escorting the Iraqi rebel forces to the Iranian border. In so doing, the Kings hope that American viewers will recognize the righteousness of their endeavor and support the Kings despite their treasonous actions. The three hope subsequently to use this public support during their courts-martial. The U.S. Army catches up with the Kings just as they reach the border and attempts to arrest them before their charges are freely across. In a last-ditch effort to ensure the rebels' safety, Gates, Elgin, and Barlow reveal that they have obtained the Kuwaiti bullion and appeal to the vanity and upward mobility of the commanding officer in charge of their arrests to let the rebels escape to Iran. During the closing credits viewers learn that Cruz later helped obtain the Three Kings' honorable discharge and that the Kings, having stashed some of the gold, used it after their discharges to embark upon civilian lives that are only slightly more glamorous than their prewar ones. Gates and Elgin, in fact, have gone to work in Hollywood.

These developments satisfactorily conclude the plot, but they do so by pitting the Three Kings against the U.S. military, effectively outside the conferring realm of soldier-hero status. This resolution necessitates (and explains) the film's tagline, but the film's decidedly capitalist appeal, its status as the first Persian Gulf War movie, and civilian American democracy all resist the stars' signifying function as kings. After Vietnam war movies demand heroes, especially war movies with Russell's revisionist aims. But the Three Kings' entrepreneurial impulse seems incompatible with traditional soldier-hero actions, and even discerning which three number as kings is complicated throughout the film. In fact, were it not for the film's release poster depicting Clooney, Wahlberg, and Ice Cube, viewers might have differing opinions. In his DVD commentary Russell identifies the opening-sequence party as the first time "the three" are all together, but this trio consists of Wahlberg, Ice Cube, and Jonze. From thence the film portrays sometimes three and sometimes four soldiers on the quest for the Kuwaiti bullion, and the title thus foreshadows one soldier's end. When Barlow is captured, it appears he will be the unlucky soul. Tellingly, when Gates,

Elgin, and Vig rescue Barlow, reuniting the four, an Iraqi sniper shoots and kills Vig. By convention of the war narrative, Vig seems the obvious choice to die, given his dim wits (he recalls Witt from *The Thin Red Line* and other naive forebears), his desire "to be Troy Barlow," and the movie's poster. But he's also the character who rewrites the lyrics of the title's Christmas carol to reflect a venture he will not live to complete.

Despite Russell's hopes of reworking public conceptions of the First Gulf War, this indeterminacy about whether the kings are heroes and the cleanliness of Vig's foreshadowed end blunt the film's achievement of subversive effects, and it becomes an antiseptic Hollywood action film. In *How Hysterical* Erin Runions argues that the film's excesses of effects and action plotlines, remarkably healed at the closing, "are mobilized in ways that urge the viewer to forget the violence of the U.S. attacks on Iraq through identification with a messianic position that is bound up in the film with the humanism, colonialism, and commodity fetishism that bolster, rather than resist, American imperialism" (67). And Kitaeff quite rightly argues that "the film's very critique of U.S. Military intervention in the Persian Gulf War ultimately remains limited to expression in neocolonial terms, and any critique is further undermined by the film's use of mainstream U.S. cultural and cinematic themes" (3). Indeed, Kitaeff labels the kings "outlaw heroes" (6). Marjorie Baumgarten offers a review of the film that not only deflates any of Russell's hoped-for revisionist potential but also effectively forces an understanding of the movie entirely imbued by representations of the Vietnam War, in this case *Apocalypse Now*. Baumgarten writes: "*Three Kings* has more in common with *Apocalypse Now* than with *Kelly's Heroes*, using its premise of the renegade U.S. soldiers' search for Saddam's stolen gold much like Coppola used Captain Willard's trek upriver to find Colonel Kurtz. Both movies' frameworks provide their heroes with missions that help guide us through the wars' madness and pose moral dilemmas about the intentions of the order-givers and the expression of free will." By explaining *Three Kings* in terms relative to *Apocalypse Now*, Baumgarten unwittingly participates in the First Gulf War's rescripting as another Vietnam and deftly signals public inability to understand the latter conflict other than in terms of the former.

What these critical appraisals universally overlook in attempting to account for the subversive potential of *Three Kings*, however, are images of men who compromise their fortunes when confronted with the typically American impetus to assist the downtrodden. Because of their subversive potential these men must meet containment within narratives uncannily reminiscent of those Boose notes were employed to stem "the Vietnam syndrome" in the American imaginary and in critical appraisals of them—such as those offered by Runions, Kitaeff, and Baumgarten—that refuse to call their sedition heroic. If Operation Desert Storm had successfully served to remedy "the Vietnam Syndrome," Fussell's paradigm and Scarry's structure of war would demand that postwar productions present rescued notions of heroic masculinity that had been vitiated by the previous conflict. Viewers of *Three Kings* discover that this rescue can only be accomplished via familiar narrative strategies that obfuscate immoral actions (killing of innocent civilians, reckless plundering of Iraqi resources, rampant entrepreneurial capitalism) within the broader trajectory of American goodness and beneficence (the good mission gone bad, assistance for the Iraqis disempowered by American withdrawal from the desert). Unlike representations of Vietnam, however, *Three Kings* presents a bifurcation between military venture and the entrepreneurial plundering accomplished by the film's leads. From Gates's initial "I don't even know what we did here" to the film's closing near-arrest sequence, the military venture and military leaders, with the exception of the Kings, are depicted as flawed, undoubtedly an inheritance from the previous conflict and from *Catch-22*. Against this bungled enterprise Russell casts the Kings to seek their own adventure in a traditional action plot, but the elements of that plot—theft, murder, sedition—do not jibe with traditional soldier-hero masculinity—hence the critical compunction to label the Kings as antiheroes or outlaw heroes.

Even though their images of manliness might be recognizable for *men*, the Three Kings' categorization as anti- or outlaw represents societal reluctance to adopt the new definitions of masculinity for *soldiers* and echoes the sentiment of the song lyrics serving as an epigraph for this section. Joshua Goldstein argues that "the Gulf War created a 'new paradigm of manhood' for Americans . . . that negated the loss of manhood in the Vietnam War. The central element of the new manhood was its 'slight feminization' through the addition of tenderness to the traditional tough and aggressive version of manhood" (279). Certainly, the men of *Three Kings* portray the changes Goldstein describes: they side with and support the enemy, traditionally read as feminine, in what turns out to be a largely humanist enterprise, though admittedly for capitalist purposes. Though all Hollywood megastars, none of the principle Kings of the movie embodies the tough, aggressive pose thought to accompany the masculine soldier-hero, à la John

Wayne: George Clooney was made famous portraying an emergency room doctor on NBC's *ER*; Mark Wahlberg rose to fame through a series of highly revealing underwear commercials for Calvin Klein that depicted him as the traditionally feminized object of the erotic gaze, depictions the film recalls in Wahlberg's shirtless scenes; and Ice Cube's masculinized sneer is nothing if not recognizably forced. Yet only Marjorie Baumgarten argues that "*Three Kings* shows how sedition can, indeed, be an act of heroism," so for most viewers no revision of the conflict emerges, and certainly no new definitions of men.

The great irony of Russell's movie emerges, then, because its subversion of traditional masculinity occurs within the framework of rescuing Vietnam: because, being traitors, they cannot be heroes, these Kings are only acceptable *as men* because they demonstrate the moral rectitude, the justness, of their cause, but even this decidedly American appeal is not enough for most to label them heroes. I would argue, with Baumgarten, that the men in the film are, in fact, heroic, fully aligned with Goldstein's summary of Gulf War imagistic changes, and that these images correspond to changes wrought in definitions of masculinity postfeminism. American culture simply has not yet acclimated, and the gap between civilian understanding and the soldierly experience thus emerges yet again. The reticence to view these characters as heroes (instead of as antiheroes, outlaw heroes, or kings) underscores the inefficacy of the narrative closure Operation Desert Storm offers for Vietnam—the guys may be good, but the war is not. This conclusion elicits the Vietnam syndrome all over again. Offering Boose's other focus—strictly upon the individual American soldier—Anthony Swofford's *Jarhead* similarly posits images of masculinity not yet tenable for American culture, so it too becomes imbricated with the war Operation Desert Storm was meant to complete.

## "We Don't Need Another Hero": Anthony Swofford's *Jarhead*

**All the children say**
**We don't need another hero.**
—Terry Britten and Graham Lyle, "We Don't Need Another Hero" (1986)

In her review of Anthony Swofford's *Jarhead*, Elisabeth Piedmont-Marton recounts a publicity stunt that most assuredly justifies Marilyn Wesley's statement that "war stories are not secondary reflections about war but part of its essential operation" (91). Piedmont-Marton indicates that the memoir "was scheduled for an April 4 release, but as preparations for [Operation Iraqi Freedom] escalated in the spring of 2003, Scribner moved the publication up by several weeks." Even if Scribner altered *Jarhead*'s release only on the premise that war would soon be a hot topic, the move to make the book's debut concurrent with the war's outset at least invited readers to see the "new" war in terms of its predecessor. At the most the stunt actively encouraged cultural melding of the two conflicts into one and suggested continuing American resistance to scripting the ends of wars before their beginnings.

Reviews of Swofford's memoir, likely propelled by Anthony Swofford's status as veteran of not only the First Gulf War but also the Iowa Writers' Workshop, almost uniformly praise its composition, often in relation to earlier war writing. Eager to place *Jarhead* among its forebears, Michiko Kakutani, writing in the *New York Times*, describes the memoir as "a book that combines the black humor of *Catch-22* with the savagery of *Full Metal Jacket* and the visceral detail of *The Things They Carried*." Likewise, John Gregory Dunne, writing in the *New York Review of Books*, clearly finds Swofford's memoir deserving of its literary inheritance, though one wonders whether Dunne's description of the prose constitutes compliment. Dunne writes that "without war there would be no war stories, and *Jarhead* is one of the best— loopy, stoned, its prose like three heavy metal bands playing three separate songs at once." Also in the *New York Times*, Mark Bowden, author of *Black Hawk Down*, calls *Jarhead* "some kind of classic, a bracing memoir of the 1991 Persian Gulf War that will go down with the best books ever written about military life." Though Bowden never mentions Tim O'Brien's book of the same name, by titling his review "The Things They Carried," in one fell swoop Bowden alludes to the First Gulf War's encoding within Vietnam paradigms and parlays *Jarhead*'s canonization.

Citing these self-same reviews, Piedmont-Marton says that "this kind of language had me checking the dust jacket to make sure I read the same book." Piedmont-Marton recounts that when reading *Jarhead*, she "liked parts of it a great deal, admired parts, but felt in the end skeptical and distrustful." Reflection seems only to have enhanced these thoughts for Piedmont-Marton, who ponders "the differences between [her] readings and the mainstream's reviews and commentary." Calling critical response to *Jarhead* "so skewed and hyperbolic," Piedmont-Marton argues that the response "seems to participate more in a discourse of desire than a discourse of critique." Reviewers, she claims, "really need to love this book." But, she continues, "it's simply not that good." All told, Piedmont-Marton admits to having "found the narrative voice derivative and self-involved, and the style sometimes mannered and MFA-ish and sometimes gratuitously swaggering and crude."

Though I absolutely agree with Piedmont-Marton's sentiments about Swofford's memoir and share her reaction to its reception, my purpose here is not to argue against *Jarhead*'s place in the canon of war literature. Rather, I wish to fully delineate the culture of desire Piedmont-Marton identifies as itself a product of the historical renarrativizing that the First Gulf War was meant to accomplish for Vietnam—in other words, as part of what Elaine Scarry calls the "essential structure" of war. To be, at long last, finally finished with Vietnam, Americans need the satisfaction of closure in representations of Operation Desert Storm (including *Three Kings*), a closure that critics arguably attempted to create by placing *Jarhead* in a literary lineage of great war literature—literature that's ostensibly written only about great wars. But for Operation Desert Storm to have "worked" to close out both itself and Vietnam, readers of *Jarhead*, like viewers of *Three Kings*, must accept the traditionally nonheroic images of soldiers the texts present. So pervasive is the American need for this closure that, as I argued above, *Three Kings*' anti- or outlaw heroes are contained within a traditionally recuperative narrative of American beneficence, while *Jarhead*'s "derivative" and "self-involved" narrative voice is drowned out by cacophonous praise of the memoir's literariness, praise that emerges more out of what critics want to see than what they do. Moreover, in both texts the cost is the historical marking of the war itself, a purchase that does not bode well for the United States' ability to critique and hence complete the structure of the First Gulf War, itself designed to liberate America from the clutches of the Vietnam syndrome.

The three-step process—training, execution, critique—that Paul Fussell finds integral to the "paradigm" war memoir does not unfold quite so neatly in Anthony Swofford's *Jarhead*. Perhaps because "critique" involves a complex process of reflection, in which past moments refigure in present recollections of them, or perhaps because characteristics of postmodern fractured narration and the blending of varied historical moments permeate even the memoir, locating each of Fussell's steps in *Jarhead* demands itinerant moves back and forth in the text. But this is not to say that such steps aren't identifiable in the memoir: they just seem less developmental than momentary. For the purposes of discussion of Swofford's work, I'd like to assign different labels to each of Fussell's steps, labels that I think accurately honor Fussell's model while also enabling a discussion of *Jarhead*'s texture without demolishing its shape. Because in many respects Anthony Swofford's life constituted his training for the military, in place of Fussell's "training" I'll examine Swofford's reasons for joining the U.S. Marine Corps. His actual recollections of training, which comprise a good portion of the memoir, seem in keeping with popular cultural and literary images and therefore unremarkable, though they'll receive passing mention. The execution portion of Swofford's Gulf War, because it was so brief, also coincides, at least in reminiscence, with Swofford's reevaluation of his own investment in the marines and in war. Hence, instead of simply recounting Swofford's execution of his part in Operation Desert Storm (or the lack thereof), I'll use his participation, as the memoir itself does, as a means to explore his realizations about men and war, which occur simultaneous to the war and undergird *Jarhead*'s postwar critique of the heroic compulsion to war.

*Jarhead* begins with a present-day anecdote in which Swofford unpacks the marines' Gulf War rucksack that he has stored undisturbed in his basement for a decade. Grains of Arabian Desert sand sifting from the sheaves of a map of Southern Kuwait ostensibly trigger the memories to follow. Swofford discovers that his desert camouflage suit no longer fits and explains his object-initiated reverie by declaring, "I am not well, but I am not mad. I'm after something. Memory, yes" (1). Swofford appears also to be "after" other war literature, as this anecdote references Hemingway's Harold Krebs in "Soldier's Home," whose ill-fitting uniform indicates his distance from the war, and Michael Herr's description, in *Dispatches,* of a colonial map of Indochina he finds hanging on the wall of a hotel room and that he then uses to launch his recollections. Swofford returns to this catalyst setting near the end of *Jarhead* and thus effectively, if not believably, frames both a moment of reminiscence and the structure of retelling.

This opening sequence also contains reference to Swofford's adolescent drive to join the Marine Corps, a compunction that begins to emerge when Swofford writes, "I remember about myself a loneliness and poverty of spirit" (3). Swofford expresses this loneliness at several points throughout *Jarhead,* so readers come to understand that the youthful Swofford was driven by an immense need to belong, a need he's confident the marines will fulfill. Because "it was not cool to want to be in the military," and because he's certain that his want "would be ridiculed and tainted by the kids smarter and hipper and better dressed, the better athletes, the better students, the kids who'd fucked already, the punk rockers and the metalheads" (131), Swofford keeps the desire secret, only wearing his Marine Corps t-shirt when it can be concealed. In a move accentuating his loneliness, Swofford labels those from whom he'd keep his secret "groups to which [he] could never belong" (131). Sadly, for Swofford, such groups also include his family. At one point Swofford says, "I joined the Marine Corps in part to impose domestic structure upon my life, to find a home" (145). That home appears to exist among the men of his family. Swofford writes, "I'd enlisted in the Marine Corps in order to claim my place in the military history of my family," but he says that "this initial impulse had nothing to do with a desire for combat, for killing, or for a heroic death, but rather was based on my intense need for acceptance into the family clan of manhood" (203). Though appearing rather late in the memoir, Swofford's connection between military service and manhood, once stated, lends a certain coherence to the text and places the memoir solidly within the tradition of war stories. As Marilyn Wesley states, "stories of war link the ideals of particular communities to the promise of male maturity and masculine empowerment" (83).

But the promises of masculine power no longer seem viable, given the tone of Swofford's reflection upon his experience, so the images presented throughout may point, for some readers, to the madness Swofford's opening sequence is so quick to demur. Granted, like many boys, Swofford recollects an initial draw to the weaponry of war: "For many years I felt inferior for never having fired a shotgun or large caliber rifle" (127). And he understands war's man-making potential in the culture's imagination. He calls himself "a boy falling in love with manhood" who "understood that manhood had to do with war, and war with manhood," which meant that "to no longer be just a son, [he] needed someday to fight" (128). Yet somewhere, literally on the road to his initiation into manhood, Swofford realizes that he's made a grievous mistake in subscribing to the time-honored correlation between masculinity and war. Swofford recounts that "at a breakfast stop in Bakersfield," while he's traveling to basic training at Camp Pendleton, he "considered fleeing" but decided that his "lot" was "to serve" and that he "would handle it like a man" (46). Initially, this steadfast resolution appears fully aligned with traditional definitions of masculinity, including those that attach honor, a traditionally male virtue, to service.

Curiously, however, an acquiescence to brutality, rather than the warrior's honorable "stand and fight," characterizes Swofford's induction to the Marine Corps, and Swofford appears to enjoy, rather than merely endure, his rite of passage. During one sequence the memoir recounts at length, the young recruit Swofford finds himself singled out as his training unit's scribe, a job he feels fit for, given his penchant for writing. As luck would have it, however, the scribe's actual task involves drawing a diagram of the appropriate organization of the soldiers' footlockers, not writing anything. Once his drill instructor, named only Burke, discovers Swofford's indecipherable drawing, he proceeds to harangue Swofford by "[bashing] the brim of his Smokey Bear" into Swofford's nose and slapping him on the back of the head. Swofford then recollects that "as though slowly contemplating some further violence . . . [Burke] shoved my head into the chalkboard" (29). Swofford's head breaks through the chalkboard and only stops when it reaches the cinderblock wall on which the board hangs.

In one of many moments in which the memoir recalls a scenario and then comments upon it in Swofford's purportedly present-day voice, Swofford returns to the chalkboard incident and to Burke, writing: "Now when I consider him and his acts of violence, they seem petty, not severe enough. I wish that that night at the chalkboard, after he'd shoved my head into the wall, he'd have put me to the floor with a swift knee to the stomach, followed by a boot to the face, and another boot, and that he'd have continued beating me, while the other recruits watched, horrified, observing their future. Perhaps this is only the luxury of distance and time and the reemergence of the blind stupidity and dumb loyalty that first led me into the Corps. . . . But a further beating wouldn't have damaged me, a further beating wouldn't have caused me to run" (30). Much bears observation in this paragraph. First, Swofford's motives seem obfuscated. While elsewhere they're readily described as focused on the prospect of deserving his family lineage, here they're "dumb loyalty." Second, the desire for more beating expressed at the outset of the paragraph, itself seemingly a product of reflection instead of an immediate reaction, Swofford later admits to be ineffectual. Swofford emerges, then, as a masochist, at best, and with a death wish, at worst.

This wish looms large when, upon the Marine Corps' discovery that Burke also abused other recruits, Swofford reports his beating to superiors.

Swofford writes: "I hoped that reporting Burke's brutality might somehow put me in danger, increase the odds against my survival, that his fellow DIs [drill instructors] would fuck me further and longer than anyone else, and I welcomed this imagined challenge" (31). Another such challenge highlighting Swofford's death wish occurs when he eagerly commences sniper training, urged on because the snipers are men "who gladly took on poor odds and likely death to fulfill thankless missions" (58). Swofford clearly expresses his attraction to the sniper's role: "I wanted a thankless mission," he says; "I wanted poor odds and likely death" (58). Because Swofford swears that he will not desert the marines, merciless beating and/or death appear the only escapes from "the ghastly end that awaited" him (37). The diction here, when coupled with the death-wish masochism pervasive throughout, seems a bit overblown and melodramatic, tension for the sake of the story, until Swofford recounts "placing the muzzle of my M16 in my mouth and tasting the cold rifle metal and the smoky residue of gunpowder" (70) once he is stationed in Kuwait during Operation Desert Shield.

Swofford foreshadows this scene by informing readers of his sister's lifelong battle with suicidal depression, a battle punctuated by numerous half-hearted attempts at suicide. Because of her repeated, unsuccessful attempts, doctors and statistics on suicide convince the family that "she is not serious about ending her life but is only in the throes of a cry for help because she is a woman and she is in the corner trying pills, yet again" (66). The only differences between Swofford and his sister in these parallel scenes are gender and the gun, so one wonders whether Swofford too is "only in the throes of a cry for help" in *Jarhead*. Or if what he cannot say, because he doesn't succeed at suicide when his buddy Troy stops him from using the M16, is that he's not a man by his own formulation.

And manhood seems absolutely at stake throughout Swofford's training for the marines and in his contemplation of his own bravery while waiting for Desert Storm to begin. His acknowledgment that joining the marines will not assuage his felt need thus leads him to transfer his hopes for masculine achievement onto the war itself. He writes: "I was in the stink and the shit, the gutter of the Marine Corps, the gutter of the world, and I knew I had made a mistake, but perhaps I'd discover ME in the gutter, perhaps I'd discover ME in the same way centuries of men had discovered themselves, while at war" (51).

The shift from Desert Shield to Desert Storm, from training to execution, ought to then provide the experience of war and its attendant conferring of manhood for Swofford and his fellow grunts. And certainly, as Swofford recalls, many of them experience the rush of battle, after agonizingly boring months simply waiting in the desert for war to start. Shortly after Swofford's unit learns that it has been activated, one of Swofford's colleagues jubilantly tells him, while handing him a bottle of whiskey, "Hit it Swoff, we're at goddam war" (179). Their action doesn't commence, however, until the next day, when, while digging protective trenches, the unit experiences incoming bombing (which turns out to be friendly). Swofford reacts to this initiation in a less than excited manner: "I begin to weep inside my gas mask, not because of fear . . . but because I'm finally in combat, my Combat Action has commenced." He also notes that, once again, "I've pissed my pants" (190), but refuses to acknowledge whether fear of the bombs or immense relief triggered his release.[9]

But what emerges initially as relief for Swofford quickly dissipates, to be replaced by the futility Swofford felt before his war began. His only proximity to battle occurs when he and his sniper partner, Johnny, get orders to shoot any Iraqi Army officers near Ahmed Al Jaber Airfield. The moment they request a shot, they are halted by the commanding officer of the Fox Company, who proceeds to order his company to assault the airfield while Johnny and Swofford watch from a distance (231). Because this single day of remaining spectators comprises Swofford and his unit's war experience, they're left to ponder, dejectedly, what has transpired. While his fellow soldiers "celebrate the end of our little war" (235), Swofford, in a tone of regret, says, "I feel not like a brave and proud and stupid man, but a lucky man, who showed up at the war a boy, with enough training to keep him just ahead of the battle and enough sense to keep him somewhat detached, because the war has been mine to fight but not mine to win or lose, and I know that none of the rewards of victory will come my way" (232–33). In this passage Swofford begins to process his war experience and engages in Fussell's critique of it. Inherent to that critique and inextricably linked are concepts of victory and definitions of manhood. Swofford gets no satisfaction from the victory attained and feels only lucky to have survived the conflict that, at least as his memoir condenses it, never really threatened his safety.

Swofford's lack of satisfaction leads, in the closing pages of *Jarhead*, to a questioning of his war experience: "The months of training and deployment, the loneliness, the boredom, the fatigue, the rounds fired at fake, static targets, the nights of firewatch, and finally the letdown, the easy victory that just scraped the surface of a war—all of these are frustrating and nearly unendurable facets of our war, our conflict. Did we fight? Was that combat? When compared to what we've heard from fathers and uncles and brothers about Vietnam, our entire ground war lasted as long as a long-range jungle patrol, and we've lost as many men, theater-wide, as you might need to fill two companies of grunts" (239). Swofford's dissatisfaction, elsewhere categorized as a realization of "the dark futility of the entire venture" (181), highlights the many issues *Male Armor* addresses regarding the soldierly experience of war and, more specifically, Operation Desert Storm's position within the American cultural imaginary. Because Swofford cannot fit his experience into received images of Vietnam, he indicates both how the Gulf War has not remedied (much less matched) the prior conflict and how modern, corpseless war does not fulfill for soldiers the promise war has long held for masculine achievement.

*Jarhead* specifically addresses questions about how war makes men, though Swofford couches them in terms of the marine's identity. He confirms that "to be a marine, a true marine, you must kill" and notes that this cognizance leads a marine to "sometimes . . . wish you'd killed an Iraqi soldier" because "you consider yourself less of a marine and even less of a man for not having killed while at combat" (247). Swofford's intriguing shift to the second-person point of view inculcates the reader, presumably a civilian public, in the equation of killing and manhood, while also shifting the memoir's focus off of Swofford, who never asks, "Am I a man?"

As Swofford distinguishes among civilian definitions of victory and successful male function, and his experience of personal satisfaction (or lack thereof), readers begin to comprehend that the "something" that Swofford was "after" as he commenced these reflections eludes him still, was perhaps never to be found in war at all. Swofford clearly indicates that any public recognition for his service does not suffice. He says that "the fighting man receives tokens—medals, ribbons, badges, promotions, combat pay, abrogation of taxes, a billet to Airborne School—worthless bits of nothing, as valuable as smoke" (233). And when his unit returns home to a massive parade celebrating the victory, Swofford claims that he "became bored with the routine and frustrated with the identity, the identity of the hero forced upon me" (250). He recalls "pictures from World War II victory parades in New York City" and decides that "our twenty yellow buses rambling through the high desert were a letdown in comparison."[10] The ultimate incompatibility of World War II and Gulf War imagery signals the end of "victory" as a signifying function for returning Gulf War veterans, though not for civilians, who, Swofford claims, only "want to hear the crowd-roar of victory" (245). Interestingly, one spectator attests to victory's continued signification for civilians as he hops aboard the returning soldiers' bus. The soldiers immediately recognize him as "a hard Vietnam vet . . . obviously on and off the streets for many years, in and out of VA hospitals" (250), and Swofford thus reproduces the image his own war was meant to jettison from cultural iconography. The vet proceeds to thank the servicemembers "for making them see we are not bad animals," effectively summarizing civilian expectations for the First Gulf War. Moved, but not made to feel appreciated, Swofford says, "I hope that even though the spectacle of the excited citizens was worth nothing to me, it might help the Vietnam vet heal his wounds" (251). While in some sense this passage indicates the degree to which Operation Desert Storm provided the closure military planners sought, Swofford's personal rejection of that closure suggests that the First Gulf War created a cadre of soldiers who feel precisely the same isolation as their forebears because of the gap between their experience and the culture's expectations, even if they feel it for different reasons than this ragged Vietnam veteran.

Because of this cultural desire for victory, Swofford's personal need for something else that war has not provided emerges in the text as whininess, as the derivative and self-involved narrative voice that Elisabeth Piedmont-Marton notes. Certainly, readers quickly recognize the tone. One poster to the military Web blog "One Hand Clapping," who identifies him- or herself as "a retired Army Sergeant First Class," says, "I read *Jarhead* a few years ago, and my reaction to it can be summed up easily: 'What a whiner'" (Sensing). Moments that seem self-pitying do emerge in the text. For instance, Swofford's early foreshadowing of a "ghastly end" (37) does not materialize, unless the narrative frame itself constitutes something "ghastly." Arguably, a thirty-something former marine trying to recapture his heroic moment by squeezing unsuccessfully into a uniform fitted during his peak physiognomy might indeed be ghastly.

I would suggest, however, that rather than the complaining narrative voice, the ill fit between soldierly experience and civilian expectation figures in *Jarhead*'s seemingly unjustified shift to an antiwar stance near the memoir's end.[11] Swofford claims that "the men who go to war and live are spared for the single purpose of spreading bad news when they return, the bad news about the way war is fought and why" (253), and he insists that he's "entitled to despair over the likelihood of further atrocities" (254). Another contributor to "One Hand Clapping" remarks that Swofford's depicted inability to find meaning in his experiences (admittedly not entirely accurate) "is not what any other person would find after being in that war" and that "failing to find 'meaning' is just a sign of one's pathetic inability to be a man" (Sensing).

Perhaps the "something" that Swofford's "after" involves his "pathetic inability to be a man," but *Jarhead*, like all of the other war texts studied throughout *Male Armor*, presents the soldier's experience of war as *not* matching civilian expectations of what makes a man, and though Anthony Swofford does not ask his readers to reconsider their definitions of a man, he does require them to see those they would call heroes as deeply troubled by their war experiences; as soldiers wounded in the heart; as whiners justified in complaining about their "cheap, squandered lives" (11). Because, as Swofford notes near his conclusion, "More bombs are coming" (254). And though the narrative voice is derivative, though the memoir attempts to mimic its predecessors and elevate itself to their status as iconic canonized art, and though the shift to an antiwar stance seems simplistic and forced, *Jarhead* does, like it or not, deftly inherit the tradition reviewers long to place it within. *Jarhead* thumbs its nose at those who would complain of its lack of artifice while missing its message: "Some wars are unavoidable and need well be fought, but this doesn't erase warfare's waste. Sorry, we must say to the mothers whose sons will die horribly. This will never end. Sorry" (255).

So Swofford becomes one of the children cited in the epigraph to this section and as such reflects the music of *his* adolescence, not that of a previous generation. What Anthony Swofford is looking for, what *Jarhead* and its predecessors long for, are not new heroes, but a public that will cease demanding them.

# TIME WARP

**The fundamental theme of *Jarhead*'s portrayal of marine
life is that heroes do not exist.**
—Nicholas Provenzo, "*Jarhead:* Heroes Do Not Exist"

The concordance function at Amazon.com reveals that the three most frequently recurring words in Anthony Swofford's *Jarhead* (2003) are "marines," "know," and "war." The idea these words instantiate must emerge—if not directly, at least unwittingly or subconsciously—for readers of Swofford's text. One can imagine that as William E. Broyles set out to adapt the memoir for Sam Mendes's film *Jarhead* (2005), he tried to capture its essence, knowing full well the impossibility of a direct word-to-image transference. The marines who people Swofford's *Jarhead* do know war; they possess the attribute traditionally deemed most necessary to talk about war: they've been there.

Why, then, are they not believed?

As the epigraph to these concluding remarks, I use the passage from Nicholas Provenzo's review of Mendes's *Jarhead* ironically. Provenzo criticizes the film because it does not present heroes. I would like to suggest that Provenzo reads the film correctly—there are no heroes—but laments his realization wrongly. The film version of *Jarhead* accurately takes its cue from Swofford's memoir—there are no heroes—yet aspects of civilian culture continue to fail to grasp this message. Thus, even the latest blockbuster representation of war attests to the gap *Male Armor*'s study illuminates, and though I present this analysis as a conclusion, it is really meant as a coda or a reprise.[1] If the tone of representations of war appears to be becoming ever more exasperated and depressed, and writers like Provenzo critique this tone, perhaps the desperation exists because the public is still not heeding the message and continues to demand portrayals of heroic masculinity that finally do not obtain.

Reviews such as Provenzo's, published near the time of *Jarhead*'s 4 November 2005 release, encapsulate and highlight the function of the war-and-masculinity feedback loop *Male Armor* interrogates, now into the twenty-first century. Ironically, these reviews reveal the culture's ability to recognize the disparity between civilian expectations of men at war and the soldier's accounts of war experience, yet no thoroughgoing attempts to revise these expectations issue from the culture's recognition—Provenzo critiques the film for not providing what civilian culture requires, yet he refuses to consider the alternative: that "there are no heroes" is indeed the film's message.

The confluence of several concepts involved in the culture's misapprehension and inaction can be portrayed most vividly through the phenomenon of the time warp, hence this conclusion's title. First, reviews of the film version of *Jarhead* emerged concurrently with increasingly pressing critiques of Operation Iraqi Freedom, the United States' second Gulf War, and thus also form a part of the reflective evaluation of the previous Gulf War, Operation Desert Storm. In other words, critiques of the present serve the same function for the past in Elaine Scarry's "structure of war" and hence create the impression of uniformity between the two eras.[2] Provenzo's need for heroes might reflect concerns over the *present* Gulf War more than a critique of *Jarhead*'s historicizing of the *earlier* war. Second, Mendes's *Jarhead* itself creates an impression of contemporaneous Gulf Wars, which contributes to a sense of wartime synchronicity because of critical desire to graft the film imagistically and narratively onto the present. Third, some details of Operation Iraqi Freedom mirror so closely the personalities and events of Operation Desert Storm that a feeling of warped time emerges despite radically different prewar components and combat operations.

And finally, an uncannily familiar soldierly experience of war has reappeared in early accounts of Operation Iraqi Freedom: Nathaniel Fick's *One Bullet Away* and Jason Christopher Hartley's *Just Another Soldier*. A mere glance at these accounts demonstrates the continued bifurcation between civilian expectations and soldierly experience of war, and both express an almost defeatist mentality, a skepticism that civilians will ever grasp the gap or change their thinking about war.[3] In this conclusion I would like to briefly enumerate these facets of warped time in order to place *Male Armor*'s literary and historical investigation in an immediate context. The urgency of such contextualizing has never been so clearly metaphorized than in recent soldiers' complaints that they lack the armor to adequately protect themselves in combat ("Could Better") or in the experiences of the soldiers recounted in the "Soldier's Heart" documentary, with which this book begins. The sooner the civilian public registers its culpability in enabling the war enterprise, the sooner we can mount effective efforts to protect our servicemembers or to finally bring them home.

Enthusiastic reviews of Sam Mendes's *Jarhead* (2005) appear to either miss the film's message or pervert what vestiges of Swofford's memoir remain, while reviews castigating the film ironically recognize Swofford's aim. In both cases the assessments manifest the societal inability to apprehend the soldier's experiential critique. The reviewer for my university's daily, the *Western Herald,* lauds both the "reality" and the "truth" Mendes's film conveys. Telling readers that *Jarhead* is "definitely a movie to see, especially if you want to understand the trials and tribulations of being a Marine in a more contemporary war," Kyle Shull repeatedly references "the real experience" and "the real life" of marines, calling the film "honest and enlightening." However, Shull never pauses to articulate precisely how the film enlightens, the "truth" the film adumbrates, or the elements that make it "real," unless "trials and tribulations" are meant to suffice. Shull's review thus misses the marines' frustration with their nonwar.

Largely appraising of the film and apparently not so concerned about its truth or reality, *Newsweek*'s critic David Ansen says that "*Jarhead* gets A's for everything but its story"; this, as the title of Ansen's review indicates, is "A War Movie without a War." Unlike Shull, who only fails to articulate his meaning, Ansen seems not to have *seen* the film, even though he correctly calls it "a movie about the anticipation of war" featuring "soldiers who never get to fight." Deriding the film's "foreplay" without a "climax," Ansen presents the desire undergirding his criticism of the film: "You want those damn battle scenes!" Any reader familiar with the book recognizes that an understated though key part of Swofford's presentation involves the marines' sense that they have not experienced war, so to demand that the movie present not only a different image of war than the memoir but an alternate historical reality misses the point entirely. But most telling for the purposes of displaying the disjunction between civilian and veteran understanding, a disjunction informing Swofford's exasperated apologies near the memoir's end, is Ansen's resort to the second-person "you." "Let's be honest," he says, about what "you" want, thus raising the specter that Americans will not see the reality, the nothing that is, because it does not satisfy their desires. Ansen's complaint unwittingly identifies civilian society's demands for a visually satisfying war experience and for narratives of war not truly reflective of experiences of war. These demands civilians then foist upon young men as they retell their war stories.

This desire for an alternate visual experience of Operation Desert Storm also imbues Nicholas Provenzo's scathing critique of Mendes's *Jarhead*. Provenzo illuminates a key irony of the gap between civilian and soldierly understanding, blatantly displaying how civilian investment in a particular type of narrative about war's effects prevents accurate interpretation of the only ostensibly legitimate retelling of these effects—the veteran's. Writing for *Capitalism Magazine*, Provenzo summarizes that "what one finds in *Jarhead* are empty men who drift through life, denied of what they truly want, and who choose to make up for it in emotional outbursts and sadistic and debased pleasures. Again and again, this is what Hollywood sees when it looks at the marines." The critique of Hollywood certainly warrants consideration, as prowar films seem largely relegated to the action/adventure genre (which, one could argue, both portrays and glorifies outbursts and pleasures similar to *Jarhead*'s), and unlike Ansen, Provenzo astutely identifies what he has witnessed. Provenzo expresses concern that "no massive backlash by marines" has been fomented and amazement at "the positive reaction many marines have had," without considering either phenomenon.

I recount these reviews not to establish that upon a prompt from Swofford, Mendes tells the "real" story of Operation Desert Storm, but to suggest that the tension between what civilians expect from war and how war gets narrated in American culture, often by soldiers themselves, persists. Even rather simplistic responses to Mendes's *Jarhead*, like Shull's, though cognizant of the "trials and tribulations" associated with war, exuberantly connect yet again the brutal testing of men with truth and reality and essentially make the war experience, however ignominious, one to strive for. Such responses misread narrative depictions of war that frequently aim to disrupt war's signifying function and hence its impetus for men. Two early accounts of contemporary military life and ongoing international conflicts, Nathaniel Fick's *One Bullet Away* and Jason Christopher Hartley's *Just Another Soldier*, both chronicle a young man's attraction to the military and highlight how war remains the crucible for American masculinity. As those written during previous war eras, these narratives chart the participants' growing disillusionment with the cultural impetus to war. Yet Fick and Hartley both painfully and chillingly exhibit a sense that they should have detected war's false promise early on.

Fick's memoir embodies the "paradigm war memoir" Paul Fussell defines in *The Great War and Modern Memory* as encompassing "first, preparation; then execution; and finally, critique" (130), as Fick details his military indoctrination, training, and experience. During this narrative unfolding Fick also references elements that create the time-warp effect Operation Iraqi Freedom had for civilian Americans: the lingering effects of the Vietnam conflict on the marines. He writes: "If Vietnam still grips the nation's consciousness, its memory is doubly strong in the Marine Corps. When officers and staff [noncommissioned officers] in Iraq turned their backs, Marines were apt to slip an ace of spades into their helmet bands or write slogans on their flak jackets, 'Born to Kill,' 'George Bush's Hired Gun.' I heard Iraqis referred to as 'gooks' or 'Charlie,' only half jokingly. Vietnam Marines are still the archetypal Marines" (282). Fick's acknowledgment of Vietnam's vestiges negates any notion that Operation Desert Storm "won" Vietnam, and it signals the potential for the First Persian Gulf War's designification in or erasure from the culture's memory. These tracers also illuminate the possibility that the United States is again attempting to conclude an era.[4]

When critiquing his war experiences, Fick says, "I left the Marine Corps because I had become a reluctant warrior" (364), but he forgoes details of his departure from military service, including specific discoveries of this reluctance during his tenure. Fick closes his book by describing a trip he takes to Antietam with a childhood friend, whom he asks, "Was it a waste?" She responds by referencing the historical significance of their destination: "They freed the slaves the way you freed the Afghans." While Fick ponders her assessment, he eventually concludes that he is, indeed, proud. He says: "I took sixty-five men to war and brought sixty-five home. I gave them everything

I had. Together, we passed the test" (369). The test, of course, is the test of manhood, and in his conclusion that "we fought for each other" (369), Fick manifests what will, in reflection, become both his raison d'être for joining the military and his mode of countenancing the experience.

For Fick the "test of manhood" mode replaces another: the narrative of war's goodness. Fick's friend accurately verbalizes civilian culture's means for legitimizing a war experience—freeing the Afghans—replete with simplifications that allow for such legitimizing in the first place. For combatants, however, ledger balancing comes not so easily or readily, and Fick represents brilliantly the soldier's precarious balance at the threshold of reacclimation to civilian life. Fick describes his discomfort with civilian narratives—"The good was abstract. The good didn't feel as good as the bad felt bad. It wasn't the good that kept me up at night" (369)—and in so doing enumerates the various compromises of experience that subtend the veteran's civilian life.

What surprises in *One Bullet Away*, however, is the notion that Fick would ever find himself at this crossroads in the first place. Touted as a Dartmouth-educated marine officer (an identity Broyles accords to one soldier in Mendes's *Jarhead*), Fick reveals trappings of his bachelor's degree in classics through the memoir's textual allusions and its epigraphs, which come from Thucydides, Plutarch, and Augustine of Hippo—references likely unfamiliar to most enlisted men. But like civilians who refuse to recognize the disjuncture between their expectations of war and the narratives veterans tell, Fick appears not to have grasped the import of the writers he studied in college until after his war experience. What emerges instead are Fick's descriptions of the allure of military service, which he describes after a grueling night humping in Afghanistan: "Television commentators could pontificate from their climate-controlled studies about technology and the 'revolution in military affairs,' but on the battlefield that night, long history marched unchanged into the twenty-first century. Strong men hauled heavy loads over rough ground. There was nothing relative about it—no second chances and no excuses. It was elemental and dangerous. It was exactly why I'd joined the Marines" (134). Fick's statement most assuredly supports Alex Vernon's contention, in *Soldiers Once and Still*, that soldiers' essential activities remain relatively unchanged despite technological innovation. Of more interest for *Male Armor*'s principle investigation are the cultural or individual forces driving Fick to desire and find satisfaction in such an experience in the first place. For Fick such an experience involves feeling "tired, cold, wet, hungry," sensations he summarizes as feeling "like a Marine" (260), and this hearkens to a tradition of defining men through their capacity to endure.

In claiming that "bitching is the only truly inalienable right of the soldier" (12), Jason Christopher Hartley deflects Fick's correlation between suffering and military service. Instead, in *Just Another Soldier,* a collection of Web blog entries covering Hartley's year on the ground in Iraq, Hartley subjects the military to repeated evaluation. A long-time army reservist, Hartley initially appears to offer a corrective to notions of honorable service and some explanation for the variant reviews of Mendes's *Jarhead* (or the lack thereof). He writes: "All the stories I've ever heard from vets about returning from combat are stuff like, 'You fight for the guy next to you' or 'The friends you make in combat will be the best you ever make.' Whatever" (3). Though Hartley enjoyed his combat service—he writes that "fighting there was an incredible experience for me"—he retains little praise for his comrades, saying that "the worst part was being surrounded by so many assholes. . . . I couldn't stand them as a group" (3). These comments, especially coming so close to the beginning of Hartley's compilation, suggest an invitation for the reader to disrupt connections between war service and a man's self-actualization.

*Just Another Soldier* affords a similar possibility regarding cultural attitudes prohibiting masculine signification in the presence of homoerotic desire. Hartley, perhaps unwittingly, suggests the extent to which American culture has unlinked desires from identities, especially as they relate to sexual orientation and gender. Hartley recollects a leave during which he meets Karl, a soldier who embodies ideals of masculine beauty. He remembers how "when Karl took off his uniform blouse . . . , my mouth literally went slack. He stood a good six feet three, about an inch taller than me, and the muscles of his back hung off his neck and shoulders like enormous cuts of beef brisket." Hartley says that Karl's "elegance of form" evinced "acute feelings of fear and envy" in him (171). Hartley recognizes the import of these reactions but comfortably dismisses their implications for his sexuality. He says that "it's moments like this in a heterosexual man's life when there is a staggering confusion that comes over him as he struggles to determine if he wants to *fuck* this guy or *be* this guy" (172, emphasis in original).

Hartley's capacity to separate his potential desire for Karl from any statement about his sexuality signals the extent to which American culture in general has begun to dismantle the signifying functions that connect desires to identities, a key step in undoing problematic implications of gender and certainly a boon for the sociopolitical aspirations of Queer Theorists. Despite this very contemporary understanding of the interrelations between gender and sexuality, Hartley surprisingly still fully invests war with the capacity to validate masculinity. When he learns about how the army will outfit his unit, Hartley describes his "command [of his] own Humvee" as "the cool part" of his accoutrements. He says, "I'll be driving a vehicle in Iraq that any boy who ever watched GI Joe could only dream of" (20).

Thus, Hartley registers the ironic replaying of ideas and events shaping the daily lives of contemporary Americans—boys still want to go to war and play GI Joe. But he signals some changes with the potential to disrupt the interdependent chain of ideological investment humans use to justify and execute war—the image of the soldierly male he presents is perfectly at peace with potential threats to traditional masculine signification. On the one hand, I think we would do well to read Hartley as just another soldier and to see his bemusements as aligned with soldierly masculinity.

On the other, I ponder the effect of American civilian investment in a particular narrative of war, the narrative, like Provenzo's, that insists on war's heroic function, that raises boys who want to play GI Joe, that demands heroic behaviors of those who fight and leaves those who don't depressed by their lack. Despite how the authors examined here have written about their own war experiences, the cultural narrative of honorable war persists tenaciously, and it registers most significantly in the image of the soldier-hero who bears the brunt of founding, enacting, and upholding a narrative of national identity. Though Joshua Goldstein is certainly correct that "none of us knows the correct direction or doctrine that will end war, equalize gender, or unlink war from gender" (413), perhaps cognizance of civilian investment in the link between war and masculinity will initiate some important work in that direction. In the meantime perhaps Americans might recall that without warriors, there would be no war.

# NOTES

## Introduction

1. Though summaries of the causes and manifestations of PTSD are certainly numerous and widely available, Joshua Goldstein's *War and Gender* offers descriptions of PTSD's causes and effects that are accessible to readers without medical or psychological professionalization (260–63).

2. Pogany fought the charges down to willful dereliction of duty ("Army Drops") and was only able to clear his military record of the marks against him upon being diagnosed with abnormal eye, ear, and balance functions at the Spatial Orientation Lab at the Naval Medical Center in San Diego. His doctor there, Michael Hoffer, wrote that Pogany's symptoms likely resulted from "drug toxicity antimalarials" (Warner) and linked the toxicity to Lariam, an antimalarial taken by servicemembers in both Iraq and Afghanistan.

3. Joshua Goldstein documents that "as of 1999, nearly 200,000 women serve in the U.S. military" (87). This number constitutes 14 percent of the total force. Though women remain technically prohibited from combat positions, many would claim that they nevertheless participate de facto in combat in Operation Iraqi Freedom.

4. David Buchbinder locates such external sources for men's psychological breakdowns and contrasts them with the sources identified for women, such as hysteria. Buchbinder notes that *hysteria* derives from the Greek root *hyster,* meaning "womb" (10).

5. I do not mean for this "bridge" to elide the Korean police action or the dedication or sacrifice of those who served in Korea. I've elected to bridge the years between World War II and the Vietnam War using *Catch-22* because this text can, in retrospect, demonstrate the gap between civilian ideas about war and the soldier's experience of it, a gap I show to be extant from at least World War II onward.

I've tried to include historical aspects of the Korean War throughout the first two chapters when they constitute aspects of the civilian comprehension of war, including MacArthur's firing and POW interrogations. But theorizing the Korean War's place in American *history* is beyond the parameters of the present study, and defending the literary or cultural status of representations of the Korean War explicitly (without, e.g., claiming that such representations are "really" about Vietnam, as is the case for both the film and television series versions of *M*A*S*H*) has always proved vexing for critics. Peter G. Jones argues simply in *War and the Novelist* that no "thoughtful" (185) books about the Korean War have emerged. In perhaps the most successful attempt to include the Korean War in literary analyses of war, Alex Vernon studies the work of James Salter in *Soldiers Once and Still*. To include Salter in a developmental trajectory of twentieth-century American war writing, Vernon must lump Salter's Korean War–era writing together with his World War II–era writing to formulate a "midcentury" label, thus expressing his preference for addressing eras over the specific historical parameters of a given war. Vernon associates the authors Hemingway, Salter, and O'Brien loosely (and respectively) with modern, midcentury, and postmodern writing, even though he expresses serious misgivings about "postmodern" as a designation for any war era. So instead of conducting a broad historical survey, Vernon tries to suggest that his textual choices evidence a "continuum of argument" and calls his book a "study in the correspondence among three authors." In a review of *Soldiers Once and Still* John Whalen-Bridge questions both Vernon's methods (he suspects Vernon's desire to elevate Salter's status) and his textual choices, stating that either James Jones or Mailer would have made a better choice to establish the "continuum of argument" Vernon claims for the study (856). The consistent difficulties that readers of war literature have involving the Korean War suggest that the relationship between war representations and the police action's historical place has not been theorized sufficiently. I hope that *Male Armor*'s articulation of the persistent gap between civilian understanding and soldierly experience will provide a viable methodology for commencing such work.

6. I reference this and other changes to Swofford's text made by *Jarhead* screenwriter William E. Broyles in *Male Armor*'s conclusion, "Time Warp."

7. In his study *Soldiers Once and Still,* Alex Vernon also selects only veterans' literature, as a means of narrowing his focus, and he justifies his inclusions similarly. He is, however, cognizant of skepticism surrounding Ernest Hemingway's veteran status and knows full well that his will likely not be the last word. Like Vernon, I selected my texts not to privilege these perspectives but to delineate a manageable critical ground.

8. To my knowledge, only two studies focus exclusively on white men: Fred Pfiel's *White Guys: Studies in Postmodern Domination and Difference* and David Savran's *Taking It like a Man: White Masculinity, Masochism, and Contemporary American Culture*. Pfiel specifically links his analyses of masculinity to postmodern ideas of gender, and this works well for his purposes. My concerns in *Male Armor,*

however, involve exploring ways in which some cultural ideas about gender continue to be based in purportedly outmoded, traditional forms. And Savran's focus on the masochism inherent to white masculinity, while fascinating, approaches masculinity from its abject subject status. While the men of *Male Armor's* study do not necessarily see themselves as obtaining masculine dominance, they do not always see themselves in abject positions.

9. Stevens begins his poem "Asides on the Oboe" with the lines: "The prologues are over. It is a question, now,/Of final belief. So, say that final belief/Must be in a fiction. It is time to choose" (187).

## 1. "The Great General Was a Has-Been"

1. In his seminal study of masculinity in Hemingway's texts, *Hemingway's Theaters of Masculinity,* Thomas Strychacz argues that "successful" masculinity in Hemingway's works must always be exhibited for a public that valorizes the demonstration. Strychacz thus suggests that successful enactment of the Hemingway code of manhood is dependent upon public approval.

2. Before *The Old Man and the Sea,* Hemingway's most recently acclaimed novel, *For Whom the Bell Tolls,* had been published in 1940. In the interim dozen years Hemingway had published only *Across the River and into the Trees,* which was not well received by critics. Accounts of Hemingway's anxiety over having lost his authorial skills are numerous and convincing. See, e.g., Kenneth S. Lynn's *Hemingway* and Michael S. Reynolds's *Hemingway: An Annotated Chronology.*

3. Included here are Hemingway's World War I works, *In Our Time* (1925), *The Sun Also Rises* (1926), and *A Farewell to Arms* (1929), as well as his novel about the Spanish Civil War, *For Whom the Bell Tolls* (1940). I touch on Hemingway's various attempts to refocus civilian thinking about war throughout this chapter: one could readily argue that his war novels display the gap at the center of *Male Armor's* study. Margot Norris's excellent reading of the moral argument in *A Farewell to Arms,* in *Writing War in the Twentieth Century,* is to some degree reliant upon differences in perceptions between soldiers and civilians. See my discussion of Norris's reading of Hemingway in chapter 2.

4. For excellent recent studies of the interrelation between Hemingway's public and his personal or authorial personae, see John Raeburn's *Fame Became of Him: Hemingway as a Public Writer* and Richard Fatina's *Ernest Hemingway: Machismo and Masochism.*

5. Roeder demonstrates how commerce and industry in the United States assented to the OWI's control of visual imagery and willingly produced advertisements comparing civilian and military activities. For example, a Kimberly-Clark Corporation poster, entitled "Paper Delivery . . . 1943," juxtaposes a boy throwing a newspaper with a soldier lobbing a grenade.

6. The reviews of Mailer's novel are not, of course, universally positive. In fact, one of the most exhaustive studies of war writing extant at its time, Peter Aich-

inger's *The American Soldier in Fiction* (1976), delineates a number of the novel's shortcomings and connects them specifically to the gap *Male Armor* studies between civilian and soldierly understanding. Aichinger writes: "The glaring weaknesses of Norman Mailer's *The Naked and the Dead* derive largely from a very typical American inability to comprehend the character of the professional soldier" (49).

7. See *In Our Time* 69.

8. Part of Peter Jones's "comedy" label likely arises from his study's early date of composition. In 1975 few critical literary studies, aside from Fiedler's *Love and Death in the American Novel*, tackled homosexual desire or relationships, and certainly James Jones's presentation was among the most forward in war literature at the time. Though some of the other war novels Peter Jones studies confront homosexuality as well, few of those novels have retained the stature of *The Thin Red Line*, and most present homosexuality as pathological. The fact that James Jones doesn't in this novel (even though he had done so earlier, in *From Here to Eternity*), combined with Peter Jones's lack of a critical vocabulary for discussing homosexuality in literature, probably prompts Peter Jones to read Doll and Arbre as he does. Certainly Doll's surprise at his desire has comic undertones, but just because he fumbles with this newfound desire in funny ways does not mean that readers should view the entire pursuit and the desire that underlies it as *intended* for comedy. Perhaps the scenes are funny only because of the discomfort they create when not typically male desire permeates, and thus forces a reexamination of, typically male behaviors.

9. Over breakfast one morning while they're on a fishing trip, Bill Gordon admits to Jake Barnes that he's "fonder of [Jake] than anybody on earth." Gordon understands, however, that he "couldn't tell [Jake] that in New York" because "it'd mean I was a faggot" (*Sun Also Rises* 116). Bill fears that what Jake doesn't comprehend about America after Jake's long absence are the changes in behaviors appropriate to gender, changes that apparently would imbue the interactions between the men with altogether different significance. Like the men in Jones's novel, Bill and Jake are cognizant of divergence between civilian and soldierly expectations of masculinity and therefore of their respective understandings about war. See Blackmore.

10. I cannot escape the narrative similarities between Barr's novel and Henry James's *Daisy Miller* or Annie Proulx's "Brokeback Mountain," so artfully rendered in Ang Lee's 2005 film. Though Phillip and Tim reverse in age Daisy and Winterbourne's relationship, they match with respect to traditions. The two who would scoff at established ways, Daisy Miller and Tim Danelaw, must die. *Quatrefoil* might indeed be Barr's version of the marriage plot for homosexuals, but I do not sense that Barr's depiction of Danelaw is meant to establish Danelaw's rightful end, as James intended for Daisy. Likewise, in Lee's *Brokeback Mountain*, after nearly two decades of a catch-as-catch-can relationship, Jack is murdered at about the time Ennis Del Mar determines that the men can never be together. Though

the movie codes the murder as "wrong" by connecting it imagistically to Matthew Shepard's gay-bashing, the reverberations of the marriage plot in Proulx's story are undeniable. The examination of such narrative similarities is, however, beyond the scope of this project.

## 2. The Bridge to Vietnam

1. See chapter 4 for a detailed exposition of the traditionally nonheroic status of Russell's protagonists.

2. See the introduction, note 5, for an explanation of my decision to omit a specific chapter devoted to Korean War literature in what otherwise appears to be a study organized historically by wars. By using the label "war era," I hope to both encapsulate civilian sentiment during and after historical war periods and account for the often decadelong lag between the end of hostilities and the production or release of representations of a particular war. My intention is not to elide the Korean police action nor to gloss the sacrifices and dedication of the soldiers and support staff who served in Korea.

## 3. Envelope, Please

1. In *Soldiers Once and Still* Alex Vernon offers an important counterargument to the idea that the Vietnam conflict was categorically different from earlier American wars, an argument Vernon must forward to facilitate the convergence and unity of what he calls "veteran's literature." I concur with Vernon that to the soldiers on the ground tactics do not alter all that significantly, and I defer to his experiential perspective, but Herr's *Dispatches* frequently cites military references to and descriptions of alternative tactics and strategies, as they emerged in press briefings about events in Vietnam. I use these press-created, popular conceptions of Vietnam's difference from prior wars because public perception of war, however variant from historical or tactical reality, forms one of the principle nodes *Male Armor* investigates.

2. Jeffords also cites Herr's pronominal usage as evidence of this shift, noting that Herr moves from an individual narration utilizing the first-person singular to a narration of the collective using the first-person plural, a shift that is not maintained throughout Herr's text. In addition, Jeffords's discussion leaves out the use of the second person, as in the quote she cites in her discussion of Herr's traverse from a feminine to a masculine subject position. The second-person "you" could reasonably refer to Herr, to the collective, or to the reader. See Jeffords, *Remasculinization* 42.

3. In her review of David O. Russell's film *Three Kings* (1999), Lila Kitaeff writes of the "spiritual nature" of Ice Cube's character in the film (Chief Elgin), saying that Elgin "seems untouchable" because of it. Kitaeff suggests that such "mysterious 'good luck'" plays into discourses of the other in general and of African

Americans in particular, seen culturally as romanticized, steeped in mystery that cannot be understood, reliant on mystical rather than logical means of living." Certainly many of these attributes pertain to the African American soldiers Herr describes.

4. I am indebted to Christopher Craft for the formulation of this argument. In "'Kiss Me with Those Red Lips,'" Craft posits that the transfusions each of the male characters in Bram Stoker's *Dracula* offers to Lucy comprise a communal penetration of her that involves the displacement of sublimated homoerotic desire onto the female figure. Craft claims that this sharing becomes the only way in which homoerotic desire can exist in *Dracula* because medical necessity deems it acceptable. Also see Margaret L. Carter's *Dracula: The Vampire and the Critics*, the collection in which Craft's article appears.

5. For details about homosocial heterosexuality see Sedgwick, Rubin.

6. I am grateful to Sara Bijani for pointing out this attribute of Carlyle.

7. I wish to thank Lisa Cohen Minnick for guiding my thoughts about attitudes associated with English-language variation and for helping me find more productive ways to write about them.

8. Janet Halley raises this critique concerning the "paranoid semiotic system" (5) she detects in the "Don't Ask, Don't Tell, Don't Pursue" policy regarding homosexuals serving in the U.S. Armed Forces. Halley interrogates the policy for its vagueness and the improbability of its uniform application, claiming that "far from setting up an objective yardstick that will allow servicemembers to 'play by the rules,' the 'reasonable person' feature of the policy has made every unit with a commander intent on enforcing the policy into a paranoid semiotic system in which the signification of homosexuality and of heterosexuality are always changeable, always at stake, always electrically important" (5). Halley also foreshadows the myriad ways in which the policy may meet enforcement: "Doing things that make your commander think you are gay—like making pro-gay statements, or cutting your hair a certain way, or not fitting the gender stereotype of the sex you belong to—can be the basis for an inference that you have engaged in or might someday engage in homosexual conduct; and once your commander draws that inference you can be discharged from the military unless you can prove that you have *no propensity* to engage in such conduct" (15, emphasis in original).

Given this analysis of the policy, Rabe's play seems incredibly prescient about the difficulties of implementing and enforcing "Don't Ask, Don't Tell."

## 4. Winning This Time

1. Readings of *Rambo: First Blood II* that employ language similar to Boose's are so pervasive as to suggest that, at least in critical/theoretical accounting for the film, few competing interpretations obtain. Others articulating similar ideas include David L. Sutton and J. Emmett Winn, who also point out the relationship between Stallone's film and its message about collective American remembrance of Vietnam, and Susan Jeffords, in *Hard Bodies*.

2. I develop the argument about this mode of narrative, suggested by Lynda Boose in "Techno-Muscularity and the 'Boy Eternal'" (584), later in this chapter.

3. Both Margot Norris and Douglas Kellner specify that governmental and military control of media was designed specifically to correspond to technological innovation so as to provide the public with images of war they could support because they involved no civilian casualties, no "collateral damage." Norris writes, "The Persian Gulf War's hyperrealities were constructed out of a military press censorship whose agenda was to derealize casualties, to strip them of the impact of 'reality' and thereby make Operation Desert Storm murderously destructive, yet simultaneously corpseless" (236). As of the writing of this piece, January 2007, critical narratives of the First Persian Gulf War appear to be nearly of a piece in suggesting the management of imagery Norris recounts. The military-authored accounts of tactics and strategy, Kellner argues, emerge as nearly complete fabrications also designed to support anesthetized versions of the war (219–22). Kellner's argument that the world, in the First Gulf War, witnessed an "evolution of postmodern war" (232, note 27) will demand some revision as the tactics necessary to countermand insurgent warfare in present-day Operation Iraqi Freedom more accurately model those of traditional warfare or of Vietnam's small-unit combat and hence reinforce Alex Vernon's astute insistence on the importance of an experiential focus. That military tactics of necessity revert to traditional modes of warfare, however, essentially supports my contention that Operation Desert Storm might eventually meet both historical and narrative erasure, subsumed by the conflicts that bookend it.

4. Anthony Swofford thinks that such Vietnam-era war movies and rock music do not belong in "his" war, perhaps because of his struggle to identify what is "his" about Operation Desert Storm (213).

5. As I argue in the conclusion, this crisis of masculinity emergent in narratives of the First Gulf War, imbued by everything the war did not accomplish, subtends the War on Terror's Second Gulf War, Operation Iraqi Freedom; extends "winning big this time" to an unidentifiable point in a highly militarized future; and further confounds the signifying systems of American self-definition.

6. That the 2005 movie version of Anthony Swofford's *Jarhead* also contains a postwar party scene (though at night), despite protestations that any such revelry occurred at the finish of the war, suggests that the party scene is fast becoming de rigeur in representations of the First Gulf War. See the conclusion.

7. At the time of the film's release, rumors abounded that the crew had used an actual cadaver to film the injury sequence, but Russell denies the veracity of such stories at the end of the "Director's Commentary."

8. Though *Three Kings* marks a tangent in Russell's career (Russell returned to a character-driven feature with *I Heart Huckabees* [2004]), the story of an entrepreneurial attempt to requisition the spoils of war may not be entirely new. Lila Kitaeff locates the inspiration for *Three Kings* in the 1970 film *Kelly's Heroes* (dir. Brian G. Hutton; starring Clint Eastwood), which she claims "lacked the moral twist of Russell's film." Kitaeff also points out that "even though remakes are cur-

rently big business in Hollywood, *Three Kings'* connection to its predecessor was barely mentioned in current marketing or critical reviews." Though some reviewers do mention the connection, Russell himself has never alluded to it.

9. The subject of Swofford's repeated wetting of his pants recently surfaced in reactions posted about the 2005 movie release of *Jarhead* (starring Jake Gyllenhaal) on the military blog "One Hand Clapping." On hearsay alone one writer contends that Swofford's incontinence is one "among other absurdities" of the book, but certainly a small amount of reading in war literature reveals, at minimum, the fear of pants-wetting, at maximum its frequency.

10. Swofford's reference to World War II—a more recuperable war than its successors, especially in terms of the heroic masculinity Swofford so misses— strikes me as particularly interesting here. Swofford's brief note at the end of the text indicates that he only studied critical appraisals of the First Gulf War, not of any prior wars. But Swofford may possess more war study than he admits, because at one point in the memoir he describes how he "threw my ninety papers, with expertise, using the same aiming technique that would later help me while tossing grenades" (128). This reference uncannily models a 1943 Kimberly-Clarke advertisement that depicts precisely the scene Swofford describes—a paper boy throwing papers paired imagistically with a soldier throwing grenades (see chapter 1, note 5). George Roeder reproduces the advertisement in *The Censored War,* claiming that it signaled corporate participation in recruitment efforts for the war (72). Granted, the photographs of World War II parades Swofford cites comprise an important American iconography Swofford could have seen at any time, and Vietnam certainly featured no such parades for him to access imagistically. But the uncanny similarity between Swofford's recollection and the Kimberly-Clarke ad, coupled with Swofford's clear obeisance to earlier war writing, indicates a wider reading history in the discipline than that credited at *Jarhead*'s end. That Swofford feels compelled to hide this wider knowledge indicates to me his desperate reach toward outmoded models of masculinity. Following I indicate the incompatibility of Swofford's World War II images and his Gulf War experience. Tellingly, Swofford never reminisces about throwing a grenade, so readers must assume it was part of his training.

11. Swofford's resolutely antiwar stance emerges more forcefully in his foreword to Gerald Nicosia's *Home to War: A History of the Vietnam Veterans Movement* (2004), in which he labels Operation Iraqi Freedom "America's latest ill-advised and corrupt war" (xxiii). The foreword expresses Swofford's concern, only obliquely referenced in *Jarhead,* over the compunction to war. If he'd had access to information about the violence and atrocity of war, Swofford claims, he "might have gone to college at eighteen rather than having signed the [marine] contract" (xxi). Interestingly, in labeling Operation Desert Storm the conflict of "Southwest Asia" (xxi), Swofford not only emphasizes the interwoven narratives of the two conflicts but also nearly effaces his own, as many American readers likely expect to read about South*east* Asia.

## Conclusion

1. Since the composition of this conclusion, in March 2006, Clint Eastwood's two new World War II films, *Flags of Our Fathers* and *Letters from Iwo Jima,* have been released to wide critical acclaim. One could read the appraisals in light of general dissatisfaction with Operation Iraqi Freedom, but nevertheless, I think it bodes well that Eastwood has elected to tell the World War II story from the side of the Japanese too. His doing so may indicate that American processing of World War II is ongoing still, and this processing might include alternative views that detach definitions of soldierly masculinity from the realm of the uniquely American.

2. See chapter 4 for an explanation of Scarry's theory about how cultures conceptualize and historicize wars.

3. Though written about soldierly experiences of the First Gulf War, both Joel Turnipseed's *Baghdad Express* (2003) and Alex Vernon's *Most Succinctly Bred* (2006) evidence this same exasperated, depressed tone about civilian ability to apprehend the message of their texts. An interesting study, though beyond the parameters of this one, would examine whether or not this tone, prevalent in recent war representations, is emerging as a trope of the genre. That these two memoirs read like Fick's and Hartley's is yet another time-warp effect for me, as if we've never really stopped fighting the First Gulf War.

4. In an interview with David O. Russell that Andrew Gumbel conducted for *Los Angeles City Beat,* Russell recounts meeting George W. Bush "at the home of then–Warner Bros. chairman Terry Semel." Russell recalls: "I told W. I was making a film that would question his father's legacy in Iraq and he immediately shot back: 'then I guess I'm going to have to go finish the job, aren't I?' This was back in July of '99." While Russell and Gumbel highlight this interaction to contend that the war had long been planned, I use it to reflect the extent to which Operation Desert Storm did not complete the narrative of Vietnam, much less its own, and to establish that Americans experience the time warp largely because these events actually seem to have occurred before.

# WORKS CITED

Aichinger, Peter. *The American Soldier in Fiction, 1880–1963.* Ames: Iowa State University Press, 1975.

Anderson, Terry. *The Movement and the Sixties: Protest in America from Greensboro to Wounded Knee.* New York: Oxford University Press, 1995.

Ansen, David. "'Jarhead' Comes Up Short." Newsweek/MSNBC.com 4 November 2005. 26 November 2005 <http://msnbc.msn.com/id/9916380/site/newsweek/print/1/displaymode/1098/>.

Appy, Christian G. *Working-Class War: American Combat Soldiers and Vietnam.* Chapel Hill: University of North Carolina Press, 1993.

"Army Drops Cowardice Charge." CNN.com 6 November 2003. 7 November 2003 <http://www.cnn.com/2003/WORLD/meast/11/06/sprj.irq.cowardice/index.html>.

Astro, Richard, and Jackson J. Benson, eds. *Ernest Hemingway's "In Our Time."* Corvallis: Oregon State University Press, 1974.

Bailey, Beth. "Sexual Revolutions." Farber 235–62.

Barr, James. *Quatrefoil.* Boston: Alyson Publications, 1982.

Baudrillard, Jean. "The Precession of Simulacra." *The Critical Tradition: Classic Texts and Contemporary Trends.* 3rd ed. Ed. David H. Richter. Boston: Bedford/St. Martin's, 2007. 1933–46.

Baumgarten, Marjorie. "Three Kings." *Austin Chronicle* 4 October 1999. 25 November 2005 <http.www.filmvault.com/filmvault/Austin/t/threekings1/html>.

Berger, Maurice, Brian Wallis, and Simon Watson, eds. *Constructing Masculinity.* New York: Routledge, 1995.

Bersani, Leo. *Homos.* Cambridge: Harvard University Press, 1995.

———. "Is the Rectum a Grave?" *Reclaiming Sodom.* Ed. Jonathan Goldberg. New York: Routledge, 1994. 249–64.

Blackmore, David. "'In New York It'd Mean I Was A . . .': Masculinity, Anxiety, and Period Discourses of Sexuality in *The Sun Also Rises*." *Hemingway Review* 18.1 (1998): 49–71.

Boose, Linda. "Techno-Muscularity and the 'Boy Eternal': From the Quagmire to the Gulf." *Cultures of United States Imperialism*. Ed. Amy Kaplan and Donald E. Pease. Durham: Duke University Press, 1993. 581–616.

Bourke, JoAnna. *Dismembering the Male: Men's Bodies, Britain and the Great War.* Chicago: University of Chicago Press, 1996.

Bowden, Mark. "The Things They Carried." *New York Times* 2 March 2003. 19 November 2005 <http://query.nytimes.com/gst/fullpage.html?res=9C0DE7DC15 3DF931A35750C0A9659C8B63>.

Bronski, Michael. *The Pleasure Principle: Sex, Backlash, and the Struggle for Gay Freedom*. New York: St. Martin's Press, 1998.

Broyles, William, Jr. "Why Men Love War." *Esquire* November 1984: 55–65.

Buchbinder, David. *Masculinities and Identities*. Melbourne: Melbourne University Press, 1994.

Butler, Judith. *Bodies That Matter: On the Discursive Limits of Sex.* New York: Routledge, 1993.

———. *Gender Trouble: Feminism and the Subversion of Identity.* New York: Routledge, 1990.

Carter, Margaret L., ed. *Dracula: The Vampire and the Critics*. Ann Arbor: University of Michigan Research Press, 1988.

Chapman, Rowena. "The Great Pretender: Variations on the New Man Theme." *Male Order: Unwrapping Masculinity*. Ed. Rowena Chapman and Jonathan Rutherford. London: Lawrence and Wishart, 1988. 230–52.

Chapman, Rowena, and Jonathan Rutherford, eds. *Male Order: Unwrapping Masculinity*. London: Lawrence and Wishart, 1988.

Chauncey, George. *Gay New York: Gender, Urban Culture, and the Making of the Gay Male World, 1890–1940*. New York: Basic Books, 1994.

Cohan, Steven. "So Functional for Its Purposes: Rock Hudson's Bachelor Apartment in *Pillow Talk*." *Stud: Architectures of Masculinity*. Ed. Joel Sanders. Princeton: Princeton Architectural Press, 1996. 28–41.

Cohen, Steven, and Ina Rae Hark, eds. *Screening the Male: Exploring Masculinities in Hollywood Cinema*. London: Routledge, 1993.

Comley, Nancy R., and Robert Scholes. "Hemingway's Gay Blades." *differences: A Journal of Feminist Cultural Studies* 5.2 (1993): 116–39.

———. *Hemingway's Genders: Rereading the Hemingway Text.* New Haven: Yale University Press, 1994.

Connor, Steven. *Postmodernist Culture: An Introduction to Theories of the Contemporary*. Oxford: Basil Blackwood, 1989.

Corber, Robert J. *Homosexuality in Cold War America: Resistance and the Crisis of Masculinity*. Durham: Duke University Press, 1997.

"Could Better Body Armor Save American Troops?" Transcript. Scarborough

Country/MSNBC.com 10 January 2006. 20 January 2006 <http://www.msnbc .msn.com/id/10789839/print/1/displaymode/1098/>.

Craft, Christopher. "'Kiss Me with Those Red Lips': Gender and Inversion in Bram Stoker's *Dracula*." *Dracula: The Vampire and the Critics*. Ed. Margaret L. Carter. Ann Arbor: University of Michigan Research Press, 1988. 167–94.

Derrick, Scott S. *Monumental Anxieties: Homoerotic Desire and Feminine Influence in Nineteenth-Century Literature*. New Brunswick: Rutgers University Press, 1997.

Dibble, John C. Contribution. Scruggs 27–29.

Dotson, Edisol Wayne. *Behold the Man: The Hype and Selling of Male Beauty in Media and Culture*. New York: Haworth Press, 1999.

Dower, John W. *War without Mercy: Race and Power in the Pacific War*. New York: Pantheon Books, 1986.

Dubbert, Joe L. *A Man's Place: Masculinity in Transition*. Englewood Cliffs: Prentice-Hall, 1979.

Dunne, John Gregory. "The Horror Is Seductive." *New York Review of Books* 29 May 2003. 19 November 2005. <http://www.nybooks.com/articles/ article-preview?article_id=16296>.

Dyer, Richard. *Heavenly Bodies: Film Stars and Society*. New York: St. Martin's Press, 1986.

Easthope, Anthony. *What a Man's Gotta Do: The Masculine Myth in Popular Culture*. New York: Routledge, 1992.

Ehrenreich, Barbara. *The Hearts of Men: American Dreams and the Flight from Commitment*. Garden City, NY: Anchor Press/Doubleday, 1983.

Elliott, Ira. "Performance Art: Jake Barnes and 'Masculine' Signification in *The Sun Also Rises*." *American Literature* 67.1 (1995): 77–94.

Faludi, Susan. *Stiffed: The Betrayal of the American Man*. New York: William Morrow and Co., 1999.

Farber, David, ed. *The Sixties: From Memory to History*. Chapel Hill: University of North Carolina Press, 1994.

Fatina, Richard. *Ernest Hemingway: Machismo and Masochism*. New York: Palgrave Macmillan, 2005.

Fick, Nathaniel. *One Bullet Away: The Making of a Marine Officer*. Boston: Houghton Mifflin, Co., 2005.

Fiedler, Leslie A. *Love and Death in the American Novel*. Normal, IL: Dalkey Archive Press, 1966.

Freud, Sigmund. *The Collected Papers*. Trans. James Strachey. Vol. 5. London: Hogarth Press, 1950.

Fussell, Paul. *The Great War and Modern Memory*. New York: Oxford University Press, 1975.

———. *Wartime: Understanding and Behavior in the Second World War*. New York: Oxford University Press, 1989.

Glenday, Michael K. *Norman Mailer*. New York: St. Martin's Press, 1995.

Goldberg, Jonathan. *Reclaiming Sodom*. New York: Routledge, 1994.

Goldstein, Joshua. *War and Gender: How Gender Shapes the War System*. Cambridge: Cambridge University Press, 2001.

Gordon, Andrew. *An American Dreamer: A Psychoanalytic Study of the Fiction of Norman Mailer*. Rutherford, NJ: Farleigh Dickinson University Press, 1980.

Gumbel, Andrew. "Interview with David O. Russell." *Los Angeles City Beat* 24 June 2004. 11 November 2005 <http://www.lacitybeat.com/article.php?id=1016&IssueNum=55>.

Halberstam, Judith. *Female Masculinity*. Durham: Duke University Press, 1998.

Halley, Janet. *Don't: A Reader's Guide to the Military's Anti-Gay Policy*. Durham: Duke University Press, 1999.

Hanley, Lynne. *Writing War: Fiction, Gender, and Memory*. Amherst: University of Massachusetts Press, 1991.

Harper, Phillip Brian. *Are We Not Men? Masculine Anxiety and the Problem of African-American Identity*. New York: Oxford University Press, 1996.

Hartley, Jason Christopher. *Just Another Soldier: A Year on the Ground in Iraq*. New York: Harper Collins Publishers, 2005.

Heller, Joseph. *Catch-22*. New York: Scribners, 1996.

Hemingway, Ernest. *Death in the Afternoon*. New York: Scribners, 1960.

———. *A Farewell to Arms*. New York: Scribners, 1929.

———. *For Whom the Bell Tolls*. New York: Scribners, 1940.

———. *In Our Time*. New York: Collier Books, 1986.

———. *The Old Man and the Sea*. New York: Scribners, 1952.

———. *Selected Letters*. Ed. Carlos Baker. New York: Scribners, 1981.

———. *The Short Stories of Ernest Hemingway*. New York: Scribners, 1966.

———. *The Sun Also Rises*. New York: Scribners, 1954.

Hemingway, Valerie. *Running with the Bulls: My Years with the Hemingways*. New York: Ballantine Books, 2004.

Herr, Michael. *Dispatches*. New York: Vintage Books, 1991.

Herring, George C. *America's Longest War: The United States and Vietnam, 1950–1975*. 2nd ed. New York: McGraw-Hill, 1986.

Hewson, Marc. "The Real Story of Ernest Hemingway: Cixous, Gender, and *A Farewell to Arms*." *Hemingway Review* 22.2 (2003): 51–62.

Hightower, Jamake. *The Mythology of Transgression: Homosexuality as Metaphor*. New York: Oxford University Press, 1997.

Hopkins, Patrick D. "Gender Treachery: Homophobia, Masculinity, and Threatened Identities." *Rethinking Masculinity: Philosophical Explorations in Light of Feminism*. Ed. Larry May and Robert Strikwerda. Landham, MD: Littlefield Adams Quality Paperbacks, 1992. 95–118.

Horrocks, Roger. *Male Myths and Icons: Masculinity in Popular Culture*. New York: St. Martin's Press, 1995.

———. *Masculinity in Crisis*. New York: St. Martin's Press, 1994.

Hutcheon, Linda. *The Politics of Postmodernism*. London: Routledge, 1989.

Imamura, Tateo. "'Soldier's Home': Another Story of a Broken Heart." *Hemingway Review* 16.1 (1996): 102–8.

Irigaray, Luce. *This Sex Which Is Not One*. Trans. Catherine Porter. Ithaca: Cornell University Press, 1977.

Jameson, Frederic. *The Political Unconscious: Narrative as a Socially Symbolic Act*. Ithaca: Cornell University Press, 1981.

Jeffords, Susan. *Hard Bodies: Hollywood Masculinity in the Reagan Era*. New Brunswick: Rutgers University Press, 1994.

——. *The Remasculinization of America: Gender and the Vietnam War*. Bloomington: Indiana University Press, 1989.

Jones, James. *The Thin Red Line*. New York: Delta Trade Paperbacks, 1962.

Jones, Peter G. *War and the Novelist: Appraising the American War Novel*. Columbia: University of Missouri Press, 1975.

Kakutani, Michiko. "Books of the Times: A Warrior Haunted by Ghosts of Battle." *New York Times* 19 February 2003. 12 November 2005 <http://query.nytimes.com./gst/fullpage.html?res=9904EEDD163DF93AA25751C0A9659C8B63>.

Katz, Jonathan Ned. *The Invention of Heterosexuality*. New York: Plume Books, 1996.

Keen, Sam. *Fire in the Belly: On Being a Man*. New York: Bantam Books, 1991.

Kellner, Douglas. "From Vietnam to the Gulf: Postmodern Wars?" *The Vietnam War and Postmodernity*. Ed. Michael Bibby. Amherst: University of Massachusetts Press, 1999. 199–236.

Kennedy, J. Gerald. "Hemingway's Gender Trouble." *American Literature* 63.3 (1991): 185–206.

Kennedy, J. Gerald, and Kirk Curnett. "Out of the Picture: Mrs. Krebs, Mother Stein, and 'Soldier's Home.'" *Hemingway Review* 12.1 (1992): 1–11.

Kiernan, Robert F. *Gore Vidal*. New York: Frederick Ungar Publishing Co., 1982.

Kinney, Katherine. *Friendly Fire: American Images of the Vietnam War*. Oxford: Oxford University Press, 2000.

Kitaeff, Lila. "Three Kings: Neo-Colonial Arab Representation." *Jump Cut: A Review of Contemporary Media* 24 February 2004. 12 January 2006 <http://www.ejumpcut.org/archive/jc46.2003/kitaeff.threeKings/index.html>.

Lane, Alycee. "Black Bodies/Gay Bodies: The Politics of Race in the Gay/Military Battle." *Callaloo* 17.4 (1994): 1074–88.

Leeds, Barry S. *The Structured Vision of Norman Mailer*. New York: New York University Press, 1969.

Lehman, Peter. *Running Scared: Masculinity and the Representation of the Male Body*. Philadelphia: Temple University Press, 1993.

Looby, Christopher. "'As Thoroughly Black as the Most Faithful Philanthropist Could Desire': Erotics of Race in Higginson's *Army Life in a Black Regiment*." *Race and the Subject of Masculinities*. Ed. Harry Stecopaulus and Michael Uebel. Durham: Duke University Press, 1997. 71–115.

Lynn, Kenneth S. *Hemingway*. New York: Simon and Schuster, 1987.

Lyotard, Jean Francois. *The Postmodern Condition: A Report on Knowledge.* Trans. Geoff Bennington, Brian Massumi, and Regis Durand. Minneapolis: University of Minnesota Press, 1984.

MacInness, John. *The End of Masculinity: The Confusion of Sexual Genesis and Sexual Difference in Modern Society.* Buckingham: Open University Press, 1998.

Mailer, Norman. *Advertisements for Myself.* New York: G. P. Putnam's Sons, 1959.

———. *The Armies of the Night.* New York: Signet, 1968.

———. *The Naked and the Dead.* New York: Henry Holt and Co., 1948.

———. *Why Are We in Vietnam?* New York: G. P. Putnam's Sons, 1967.

May, Larry, and Robert Strikwerda, eds. *Rethinking Masculinity: Philosophical Explorations in Light of Feminism.* Lanham, MD: Littlefield Adams Quality Paperbacks, 1992.

McHale, Brian. *Postmodernist Fiction.* London: Methuen, 1987.

Meredith, James H. "Hemingway's Multiple Voices of War." *War and Words: Horror and Heroism in the Literature of Warfare.* Ed. Sara Munson Deats, Lagretta Tallent Lenker, and Merry G. Perry. Lanham, PA: Lexington Books, 2004. 197–214.

Merrill, Robert. *Joseph Heller.* Boston: Twayne Publishers, 1987.

Merrill, Sam. "Interview with Joseph Heller." *Playboy* June 1975: 59–76.

Meshad, Shad. Contribution. Scruggs 66–68.

Messner, Michael. *Politics of Masculinities: Men in Movements.* Thousand Oaks, CA: Sage Publications, 1997.

Miller, D. A. "Anal Rope." *Inside/Out: Lesbian Theories/Gay Theories.* Ed. Diana Fuss. New York: Routledge, 1991. 119–41.

Mosse, George L. *The Image of Man: The Creation of Modern Masculinity.* New York: Oxford University Press, 1996.

Mulvey, Laura. "Visual Pleasure and Narrative Cinema." *Screen* 16.3 (1975): 8–18.

Munder-Ross, John. *The Male Paradox.* New York: Simon and Schuster, 1992.

Murphy, Peter F. *Studs, Tools, and the Family Jewels: Metaphors Men Live By.* Madison: University of Wisconsin Press, 2001.

Norris, Margot. *Writing War in the Twentieth Century.* Charlottesville: University Press of Virginia, 2000.

O'Brien, Tim. *The Things They Carried.* New York: Broadway Books, 1990.

Pach, Chester J., Jr. "And That's the Way It Was: The Vietnam War on the Network Nightly News." Farber 90–118.

Parini, Jay, ed. *Gore Vidal: Writer against the Grain.* New York: Columbia University Press, 1992.

Pfiel, Fred. *White Guys: Studies in Postmodern Domination and Difference.* London: Verso Books, 1995.

Piedmont-Marton, Elisabeth. "Gulf War Memoir Syndrome." *Texas Observer* 12 September 2003. 7 January 2006 <http://newdev.texasobserver.org/article .php?aid1451>.

———. "Writing against the Vietnam War in Two Gulf War Memoirs." *Arms and the Self: War, the Military, and Autobiographical Writing.* Ed. Alex Vernon. Kent: Kent State University Press, 2005. 257–72.

Potts, Stephen W. *Catch-22: Antiheroic Antinovel.* Boston: Twayne Publishers, 1989.

Provenzo, Nicholas. "*Jarhead:* Heroes Do Not Exist." *Capitalism Magazine* 13 November 2005. 23 November 2005 <http://www.capmag.com/article.asp?ID=4469>.

Rabe, David. *Streamers. The Vietnam Plays.* New York: Grove Press, 1970. 2: 4–84.

Raeburn, John. *Fame Became of Him: Hemingway as a Public Writer.* Bloomington: Indiana University Press, 1984.

*Rambo: First Blood II.* Dir. George Pan Cosmatos. Perf. Sylvester Stallone, Richard Crenna, Charles Napier, Steven Berkoff, Julia Nickson, and Martin Kove. CarollCo, 1985.

Reynolds, Michael, ed. *Critical Essays on Ernest Hemingway's "In Our Time."* Boston: G. K. Hall & Co., 1983.

———. *Hemingway: An Annotated Chronology.* Detroit: Omnigraphics, 1991.

———. *Hemingway's Reading 1910–1940.* Princeton: Princeton University Press, 1981.

Roeder, George H., Jr. *The Censored War: American Visual Experience during World War Two.* New Haven: Yale University Press, 1993.

Rosen, Kenneth. *Hemingway Repossessed.* Westport, CT: Praeger, 1994.

Rotundo, E. Anthony. *American Manhood: Transformations in Masculinity from the Revolution to the Modern Era.* New York: Basic Books, 1993.

Rubin, Gayle. "The Traffic in Women: Notes toward a Political Economy of Sex." *Toward an Anthropology of Women.* Ed. Rayna Reiter. New York: Monthly Review Press, 1975. 157–210.

Runions, Erin. *How Hysterical.* New York: Palgrave MacMillan, 2003.

Sanders, Joel, ed. *Stud: Architectures of Masculinity.* Princeton: Princeton Architectural Press, 1996.

Sandison, David. *Ernest Hemingway: An Illustrated Biography.* Chicago: Chicago Review Press, 1999.

Savran, David. *Taking It like a Man: White Masculinity, Masochism, and Contemporary American Culture.* Princeton: Princeton University Press, 1998.

Scarry, Elaine. *The Body in Pain: The Making and Unmaking of the World.* New York: Oxford University Press, 1985.

Schroeder, Eric James. *Vietnam, We've All Been There: Interviews with American Writers.* Westport, CT: Praeger, 1992.

Schwalbe, Michael. *Unlocking the Iron Cage: The Men's Movement, Gender Politics and American Culture.* New York: Oxford University Press, 1996.

Scoggins, Michael C. "Joseph Heller's Combat Experiences in *Catch-22.*" *War, Literature, and the Arts* 15.1–2 (2003): 213–27.

Scruggs, Jan, ed. *Why Vietnam Still Matters: The War and the Wall.* Washington, DC: Vietnam Veterans Memorial Fund, 1996.

Sedgwick, Eve Kosofsky. *Between Men: English Literature and Male Homosocial Desire.* New York: Columbia University Press, 1985.

Seed, David. *The Fiction of Joseph Heller: Against the Grain.* New York: St. Martin's Press, 1989.

Segal, Lynne. *Slow Motion: Changing Masculinities.* New Brunswick: Rutgers University Press, 1990.

Seidler, Victor Jeleniewski. *Man Enough: Embodying Masculinities.* London: Sage Publications, 1997.

Seltzer, Mark. *Bodies and Machines.* New York: Routledge, 1992.

Sensing, Donald. "One Hand Clapping." 7 January 2006 <http:donaldsensing .com/index.php/2005/11/04/jarhead-a-review/>.

Sherry, Michael S. *In the Shadow of War: The United States since the 1930s.* New Haven: Yale University Press, 1995.

Shull, Kyle. "*Jarhead* Depicts Contemporary Warfare Well." *Western Herald* 8 November 2005: 5.

Silverman, Kaja. *Male Subjectivity at the Margins.* New York: Routledge, 1992.

———. *The Subject of Semiotics.* New York: Oxford University Press, 1983.

Simpson, Mark. *Male Impersonators: Men Performing Masculinity.* New York: Routledge, 1994.

"The Soldier's Heart." Transcript by Raney Aronson. *Frontline.* Public Broadcasting System. WGVU, Grand Rapids, MI. 5 March 2005.

Spilka, Mark. *Hemingway's Quarrel with Androgyny.* Lincoln: University of Nebraska Press, 1990.

Stecopaulus, Harry, and Michael Uebel, eds. *Race and the Subject of Masculinities.* Durham: Duke University Press, 1997.

Stevens, Wallace. "Asides on the Oboe." *The Palm at the End of the Mind: Selected Poems and a Play.* Ed. Holly Stevens. New York: Vintage Books, 1972. 87–88.

Stewart, Matthew. *Modernism and Tradition in Ernest Hemingway's In Our Time: A Guide for Students and Readers.* New York: Camden House, 2001.

Strychacz, Thomas. *Hemingway's Theaters of Masculinity.* Baton Rouge: Louisiana State University Press, 2003.

Summers, Claude J. "*The City and the Pillar* as Gay Fiction." *Gore Vidal: Writer against the Grain.* Ed. Jay Parini. New York: Columbia University Press, 1992. 56–77.

Sutton, David L., and J. Emmett Winn. "'Do We Get to Win This Time?' POW/ MIA Rescue Films and the American Monomyth." *Journal of American and Comparative Cultures* 24.1–2 (2001): 25–30.

Swofford, Anthony. "Foreword." *Home to War: A History of the Vietnam Veterans Movement.* Gerald Nicosia. New York: Carroll and Graf, 2004. xx–xxiii.

———. *Jarhead: A Marine's Chronicle of the First Gulf War and Other Battles.* New York: Scribner, 2003.

Tasker, Yvonne. *Spectacular Bodies: Gender, Genre and the Action Cinema.* London: Routledge, 1993.

Terry, Wallace. *Bloods: An Oral History of the Vietnam War by Black Veterans.* New York: Ballantine Books, 1984.

Theweleit, Klaus. *Male Fantasies.* Vol. 2, *Male Bodies: Psychoanalyzing the White Terror.* Minneapolis: University of Minnesota Press, 1989.

Thomas, Calvin. *Male Matters: Masculinity, Anxiety and the Male Body on the Line.* Urbana: University of Illinois Press, 1996.

Vernon, Alex. *Arms and the Self: War, the Military and Autobiographical Writing.* Kent: Kent State University Press, 2005.

―――. *Soldiers Once and Still: Ernest Hemingway, James Salter, and Tim O'Brien.* Iowa City: University of Iowa Press, 2004.

Vidal, Gore. *The City and the Pillar.* New York: Ballantine Books, 1948.

Vonnegut, Kurt, Jr. *Slaughterhouse-Five; or, The Children's Crusade.* New York: Delacorte Press, 1969.

Warner, Joel. "Chemical Casualties." *Boulder Weekly* 17 February 2005. 4 February 2007 <http://archive.boulderweekly.com/021705/coverstory.html>.

Weed, William Speed. "'I Love You, Man!' The Nuts and Bolts of Male Friendship." *Reader's Digest* October 2005: 108–11.

Wenke, Joseph. *Mailer's America.* Hanover: University Press of New England, 1987.

Wesley, Marilyn. *Violent Adventure: Contemporary Fiction by American Men.* Charlottesville: University of Virginia Press, 2003.

Wiegman, Robyn. *American Anatomies: Theorizing Race and Gender.* Durham: Duke University Press, 1995.

Whalen-Bridge, John. "Review of Alex Vernon's *Soldiers Once and Still: Ernest Hemingway, James Salter, and Tim O'Brien.*" *American Literature* 77.4 (2005): 854–56.

White, Kevin. *The First Sexual Revolution: The Emergence of Male Heterosexuality in Modern America.* New York: New York University Press, 1993.

Young, Charles S. "Missing Action: POW Films, Brainwashing and the Korean War, 1965–1968." *Historical Journal of Film, Radio and Television* 18.1 (1998): 49–74. <http://fornits.com/anonanon/articles/200103/20010330-258.htm>.

# INDEX

during, 73; and wars of the twentieth century, 3–4, 15, 62–63, 73, 133n5, 137n2

Kuwait, 107, 110, 117, 120

Lee, Ang, 136n10
Letters from Iwo Jima, 141n1
Life, 33
Looby, Christopher, 13
Los Angeles City Beat, 141n4
Love and Death in the American Novel (Fiedler), 136n8
Lucey, Jeff, 2–3
Lynn, Kenneth, 28–29, 135n2

MacArthur, Douglas, 15, 28–30, 133n5
Machine Dreams (Phillips), 23
MacInness, John, 8
Mailer, Norman, 6, 27, 50–51, 55, 133n5; Advertisements for Myself, 42; Naked and the Dead, 15, 36–42, 43, 45, 60–61, 135n6
Male Subjectivity at the Margins (Silverman), 34–35, 77–78
marines: in Dispatches, 82–83, 89; in Frontline documentary, 2–4; in Jarhead (Swofford), 117–24, 125; in One Bullet Away, 129–31; tour of duty periods for, 73
Martin, Jacob, 2–3, 5
Masculinity in Crisis (Horrocks), 8
M*A*S*H, 133n5
Mendes, Sam, 17, 125–29, 130, 131
Merchant, Natalie, 7
Merrill, Sam, 62
Meshad, Shad, 75
Messner, Michael, 10, 12, 20
Miller, D. A., 78
Most Succinctly Bred (Vernon), 141n3

Naked and the Dead, The (Mailer), 15, 36–42, 43, 45, 60–61, 135n6
NBC, 114
Newsweek, 127

New York City, 122
New York Review of Books, 115
New York Times, 115
Nicosia, Gerald, 140n11
1919 (Dos Passos), 36
Norris, Margot, 18, 67, 102, 135n3, 139n3

O'Brien, Tim, 70, 100, 115, 133n5
Odysseus in America (Shay), 4
Office of War Information, 15, 32–34, 39, 45, 135n5
Old Man and the Sea, The (Hemingway), 25–28, 29, 30, 135n2
One Bullet Away (Fick), 17, 126, 129–31
"One Hand Clapping," 123, 124, 140n9
Operation Desert Shield, 99, 103, 106, 108, 120
Operation Desert Storm: and Jarhead (Mendes), 126, 128; in Jarhead (Swofford), 100, 104, 116, 120–21, 122, 123, 128, 139n4, 140n11; mass media coverage of, 103, 106, 108, 109, 139n3; memoirs about, 6; and One Bullet Away, 129; and Operation Iraqi Freedom, 126, 139n3; in Three Kings, 101, 104, 106, 116; and the Vietnam War, 99–104, 113–14, 116, 122–23, 129, 139n3, 140n11, 141n4; and war technology, 105, 106, 139n3
Operation Iraqi Freedom: and film reviews, 141n1; in Frontline documentary, 2, 4; in Home to War, 140n11; and Jarhead (Mendes), 126; and Jarhead (Swofford), 114–15; in Just Another Soldier, 17, 126–27; and masculinity, 139n5; in One Bullet Away, 17, 126–27, 129; and tactics, 139n3; women in U.S. military serving in, 133n3

Pach, Chester J., 74–75
PBS, 2
Pearl Harbor, 33

**Cultural Frames, Framing Culture**

Books in this series examine both the way our culture frames our narratives and the way our narratives produce the culture that frames them. Attempting to bridge the gap between previously disparate disciplines, and combining theoretical issues with practical applications, this series invites a broad audience to read contemporary culture in a fresh and provocative way.

Nancy Martha West
*Kodak and the Lens of Nostalgia*

Raphael Sassower and Louis Cicotello
*The Golden Avant-Garde: Idolatry, Commercialism, and Art*

Margot Norris
*Writing War in the Twentieth Century*

Robin Blaetz
*Visions of the Maid: Joan of Arc in American Film and Culture*

Ellen Tremper
*I'm No Angel: The Blonde in Fiction and Film*

Naomi Mandel
*Against the Unspeakable: Complicity, the Holocaust, and Slavery in America*

Debra Walker King
*African Americans and the Culture of Pain*

Jon Robert Adams
*Male Armor: The Soldier-Hero in Contemporary American Culture*